V·E·N·I·C·E

THE FOUR SEASONS

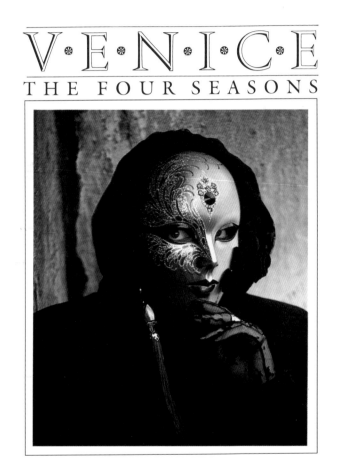

V·E·N·I·C·E

THE FOUR SEASONS

LISA ST AUBIN DE TERÁN

Photographs by Mick Lindberg

PAVILION

This paperback edition published in Great Britain in 1996 by
Pavilion Books Limited
26 Upper Ground
London SE1 0PD

First published in hardback in 1992

Designed by Andrew Barron & Collis Clements Associates

A CIP catalogue record for this book is available from the British Library

ISBN 1 85793 726 0

Typeset by DP Photosetting, Aylesbury, Bucks
Printed and bound in Spain by Arnoldo Mondadori

1 3 5 7 9 10 8 6 4 2

D.L. TO: 245-1996

This book may be ordered by post direct from the publisher.
Please contact the Marketing Department, but try your bookshop first.

CONTENTS

INTRODUCTION

'The mere thought of buying a piece of the most beautiful city in the world seemed like a sacrilege. It would have been like going to a national gallery and seeing a great Rembrandt and saying, "I'll have the painting; could you wrap it up please and send it to my hotel?"'

In a city with little space and few gardens, this wind garden has come to be one of the sights of Venice.

WHEN I first visited Venice, aged sixteen, I was so overawed by its beauty that my fleeting visit disturbed me; stirring me out of an adolescent chrysalis into something more of a literary butterfly. Many years later, I returned to Italy to live and settle there. I had been drifting, like a pirate ship in troubled waters, until then. I scoured the Ligurian coast in the faded steps of Lord Byron, hoping to find both true love and a villa. I was searching for somewhere that would satisfy my love of decaying splendour: Italy is a fine place for architectural flirting. 'Dangerous and sweet-charmed Venice' would have been an obvious choice, yet it never occurred to me to look there for a place to weigh anchor.

The mere thought of buying a piece of the most beautiful city in the world seemed like a sacrilege. It would have been like going to a national gallery and seeing a great Rembrandt and saying, 'I'll have that painting; could you wrap it up please and send it to my hotel?' Four years after I moved back to Italy, I discovered that it was indeed possible not only to rent but to buy a fragment of this priceless city. Within a month my family and I had moved there, to a corner of a convent between Santa Maria Formosa and San Marco. The gondolier who steered us to our water-gate on the Rio della Guerra called out across the intervening canals to his fellow boatman, trailing his soft-spoken dialect like the shushing of waves in his wake, 'These people are Venetians . . . *Veneziani*!'

Leaning over a silent canal, with the scent of wisteria heavy in the evening air, I thought I was in paradise. Venice has its rewards and its purgatory: it takes far more than the call of a friendly gondolier to become Venetian. There is a gruelling treadmill of bureaucracy in between, followed by the passing of the many tests needed to enter into an elitist and secret society. This book is a very personal account of Venice as seen by myself and through the eyes of my family from the inside. It does not try to guide anyone around the treasure house of the city's landmarks. It is like a view of the inside of the oyster shell by a grain of sand that has managed to lie beside a pearl.

Henry James wrote of Venice: 'There is notoriously nothing more to be said on the subject . . . . There is as little mystery about the Grand Canal as our local thoroughfare, and the name of St Mark is as familiar as the postman's ring. It is not forbidden, however, to speak of familiar things . . . .'

Since 1892, when James felt a need to apologize for adding his chapters to such an already full book, there have been dozens more dedicated to the city's temples and palaces. The buildings, though, have remained virtually unchanged. What has changed is the world around, making Venice even more unique as we move towards the twenty-first century. The flocks of half-clothed and half-starved Venetians have also changed; the ones who didn't trail yards of silk brocade in the filthy canals behind their gondolas; the ones who didn't eat off disposable gold plates. These 'starlings' have gone: migrated to America, Australia and Milan. There is a new prosperity in Venice, a welfare state independent of the sumptuous wealth of the legendary families.

Where once all visitors would have stood out as voyeurs, well-fed visitors observing their hungry hosts, it is now possible to merge with the rest of the eighty thousand Venetians with the camaraderie of a fellow Resistance fighters, defying modern times, flooding, tidal waves, pollution and the continual invasion of tourists. Until the period of initiation is over, one is treated either with indifference, suspicion or scorn. Yet it is possible now to live as most Venetians live, which is not leaning over a balcony on the Grand Canal, but somewhere in the warren of lesser grandeur, linked by its lesser canals and *rii*.

What drew me to Venice originally was the literature that had been written about her, the poetry and the letters, and the rhapsodies of pride that have been composed to her over the many centuries past. The mere name became as exotic in my imagination (and as unattainable) as Shangri-La and Xanadu. My vision of Shangri-La was shattered by the cinema and seeing the particular paradise treated in such a way that it lost its mystery and became a joke. The idea of Xanadu faded, but the vision of Venice grew, fanned by its calamities and its potential plight of a living Atlantis. Before I ever travelled to Venice, I saw her as the centre of romance.

I see in myself a tendency to sublimate a love of people with a love of place. Where I live and who else lives there has often been more important to me than whom I live with. I feel a need to embrace a place, a landscape, a village or a city in such a way that I can feel I belong there. Having grown and lived like a wandering Jew for most of my life, and having in my veins the mixed blood of so many races and nations, I often find it hard to feel other than slightly alien in any given community. My awareness of this condition, I am sure, is more to blame than anything else. But, for whatever reason, I have previously only found comfort in perpetual motion. To stay more than a few months anywhere has been, in the past, tantamount to imprisonment. This wanderlust has increased with my age; before settling in Venice, I had travelled continually for the previous five years with my children in tow. The beauty and the encapsulated decadence of Venice with all her fading elegance were what first held me to her dank bosom.

I started living here in 1988, together with the Scottish painter Robbie Duff-Scott, my (then) fourteen-year-old daughter and my five-year-old son. We seemed to have been dogged, for the two years previous to our move, by more than average ill-luck. From the moment we crossed the causeway, leaving behind the gasometers of Mestre squatting like so many giant cotton reels each threaded with a strand of gold, we found ourselves sheltered by the safety-net of the

10

T̲he waterline rots under its green slime like the hem of a fine ballgown forever trailing in puddles. Slippery steps and reflections in an encroaching frame of virginia creeper. Right: There is a sepulchral stillness about the backwaters of Venice. Slowly sinking steps and poles punctuate the shadows. Sometimes a voice or a radio interrupts the silence like a lost sea bird.

Aubergines, parsley and spinach are stacked in their crates at the Rialto market. Several mornings a week I join the shove and push of housewives competing for the finest fruits.

12

lagoon. Many of our problems thereafter were of a surreal nature only and arose from the bizarre bureaucratic hurdle race that buying property in Venice entails.

My own sense of reality and fantasy has never been particularly clear. Living in Venice has done nothing to rectify this. If anything, it has increased my habit of invention: Venetians are all historical fantasists, enmeshing the real and imagined from their past and using the concoction as a part of their present. They are illusionists (sometimes mistaken for liars, but wrongly so, since a lie implies the intention to deceive, while a fantasy is more a wish to believe). The concept of Carnival here, for example, is far stronger than its strained-for reality. The need for masks and masquerades seems crucial to the Venetians' survival, yet most of this is apparent not in the papier mâché faces that dangle from every available shop space and counter, but in the eternal, internal mirroring of the city, which is in itself a series of masks, from the splendid façades which imply a dead museum while a secret life goes on behind them, to the palaces built on water.

There used to be hundreds of wooden constructions fanned between stone walls. Most of these sites have now been cleared and rebuilt on in more solid ways. One of the last hints of these former shanty towns and pockets is the gondola boatyard. Beside a stilted wooden house, there is a forecourt over the water which comes to life each spring like an anthill kicked open and surprised.

Gondoliers used to have to survive on a pittance, but that too has changed and they make a very lucrative living, even though it is largely seasonal. They did not glide into the twentieth century, despite their practised grace. In fact, at one point their drunkenness, rudeness and cheek were so notorious they were threatened with extinction. Such troubles have passed – but there are still little boxes on walls and corners which look very businesslike and pertain exclusively to the gondoliers and actually just contain quantities of wine. Although it would be true to say that gondolas hardly every crash and their oarsmen navigate the canals with astonishing precision, I have been in a gondola in the early evening, and been in the throes of explaining their very skill to my delighted guest, when our gondola smashed into a wall.

Gondoliers inherit their jobs and mooring sites, and they are justifiably proud of their skills, which they pass on, together with their code of soft strangled cries, from generation to generation. The *centro storico* does not attempt to compete industrially – there is Mestre at the ready to spew out enough polluted smoke and fumes for both sides of the lagoon – but there are a number of family businesses of specialist artisans. One can buy a mattress in Venice that is stuffed and stitched by hand, and picture frames can be hand-carved and gilded with real gold in a workshop the size of a broom cupboard. There is little work, though, apart from tourism and service industries and the ubiquitous lace. Some of the inhabitants are artists who have, like myself, chosen to live here; many of these are foreigners, and most of them are transitory. When I settled here, three years ago, there were only ten other registered British residents. My nanny and family of four swelled that figure by fifty per cent.

The social life of Venice seems to hover around continual rendezvous which are followed by brief conversations in the street. The Piazza San Marco, the Campo San Bartelomeo and the Ponte dell'Accademia seem to be the favourite meeting-places. Each day fills like a card at a ball with appointments. These are often as brief as dances: one meets, kisses, talks, and disappears back into the alley-ways. It is as though in a threatened place there is a constant need to re-count one's friends; there is safety in numbers. Groups form and scatter through the day in a social choreography, weaving one's hours into other people's with intricacy. Outings and meals that could easily be sited without traipsing around the entire inner city rarely are. No one, no matter how old, seems to tire of circulation here. And the city is discussed and praised, nursed and nagged endlessly. There are tens and thousands of volumes on Venice in the state archives. There are tens of thousands of volumes of walking encyclopaedias on the streets. The information they gather and hoard is as varied as handfuls of air and gulps of sea water, but they all agree that Venice is the most exquisite place they have ever seen and they 'will not quit it in a hurry' if they can help it.

SPRING
CARNEVALE

'In the peeling and stained stucco of façades I see the remains of once sumptuous gowns, trailing their wet hems over slipper-like steps that rise and fall under tides to the suck and slap of canal water on the green-slimed marble.'

Left: *By day the barges ferry their goods along the narrow waterways. By night and holidays they rest, tucked up under tarpaulins.*

IT snowed again in Venice this winter. The flakes hissed into the salty canals and lay in fields in the *campi* each early morning. Instead of cars to soil its virginal white to a tea-stained slush, there are just the thin dissecting paths of pedestrians: crocodiles of green overcoated Venetians, their heads rigid above their turned-up collars, their bodies packed with layers of vests. Before them, feeting the first snow were the workmen in their anoraks and oilskins, breathing a grappa-scented cloud of air. After them will trudge the early tourists, with heads swimming on their shoulders as they gaze from façade to façade.

The previous year, when the man from SIP, the telephone company, eventually appeared to join us to 'the club of which every Venetian is a member', and install our phone, we asked him if it ever snowed in Venice. His reply was dismissive. He implied that snow was a foreign habit which the salt in the air would not allow to infiltrate here. Yet it snowed in Venice twice this winter, and to judge by the numerous postcards of the Piazza San Marco under snow and moored gondolas piled with drifts, it has snowed many times in the past. It seems that Venetians share the general Italian amnesia about weather. Once the sun appears, remembrance of the cold days is evaporated by its heat. The cold is erased, but the damp remains, with its stains creeping through paint and paper, buckling wood, and forcing chemical salts through brick and stone alike with a scattering of summer snow as fine as icing powder and as pervasive as the winter chills.

Venice is a city so orchestrated that even the seasons seem to be arranged by some expert backstage conductor. The coming of spring is no exception. The population of indolent pigeons and solitary caged canaries is swelled overnight by an influx of swallows and martins, with an occasional blackbird trilling soprano love songs in some hidden garden. The knots of seemingly dead virginia creeper that festoon walls and balconies unfurl their pink buds simultaneously from Cannaregio to Castello. The bare convent wall becomes a network of mutating reds whose changing colours synchronize with those of other similarly peeling walls: some held together, others dragged apart by the insidious kiss of the suckers of the grappling Canadian vine.

Then, honouring its continual genufluxion to the east, the sea mists that lie upon the city in winter are rolled up in spring like the carpets of the great Indian temples which are taken up and hung on the marble walls. As though by some telepathic accord, the seasonal fashions change as well. Forming part of one's own particular crocodile, traversing the city from one bar to another, usually following someone and being followed by at least someone else, everyone can be wrapped up in winter garb one night, yet all be in spring attire the following morning, and all without any perceptible change in temperature or any significant date having been reached. The Napoleonic green coat for men gives way to pristine white macs, while women sport intensely coloured hats and matching shoes, coutured suits and fancy coats. Only a small brigade of black-weeded widows ignore the changing fashion trends. A few of the old and all of the adolescents are immune. The widows cling to the mended rafts of their thick black stockings while children celebrate the early age of reason by donning the self-inflicted uniform of pale jeans, T-shirt, white socks and thick-soled shoes. For the rest, fashion is a tyrant who rules 'Let no one be different' from within the rooted class hierarchy of Venice which has already whispered 'Let no one be the same'. Thus quality and cost are constantly appraised and tests are passed or failed at every step.

Cafés and bars that have remained battened up and secret for five months suddenly spill their tables and chairs over inadequate spaces, re-dedicating their city to the great god Tourism. Cats and pigeons share the flagged spaces between stalls and chairs. The catering corps tries its luck with the same obstinacy as a rebellious child. The 'How far can I go without being stopped?' is translated into 'How much can I charge without being challenged?' As far, it would seem, and faster than the rise of the sea itself. The give and take of tourism is a sour-tasting pill that must be swallowed every day.

There are still many places in the city that have remained uninvaded. Sant'Elena, Santa Croce and the back-streets of Castello are scarcely troubled by the trudging of weary foreigners, but the emptiness of their streets attests to the change in spirit that the marching armies of sightseers have brought with them. Most of the old ladies who used to sit in their doorways making lace or just gossiping have been moved to the grey concrete apartment blocks of Mestre on the far side of the lagoon. The native population of the inner city is dwindling at a pace that outstrips natural deaths. The exodus has uprooted the old men from their lines on the street benches and it is blowing away the new generations. In this fleeting city there is little space and less earth to produce any stray dandelions, nor are there many acacias to drop their fluff and let it drift in the late spring air. The men who once sailed to Byzantium and Alexandria and a fleet of other exotic places, returning home with the rich seeds and the loot of the East, are now merely elbowed across the water. Where other places have fields of dandelion clocks to mark their wastelands, Venice has its empty doorways and uncluttered water steps. There is an encroaching neatness of halls and alleys. This is a city under siege, greeting the spring with the same relief as any ungarrisoned town would do with the enemy scaling its walls. Even the walls here are of water. Safety once lay in the treacherous lagoon where *vaporetti* now weave their way backwards and forwards to the Lido and the islands. I wonder if, when Howell wrote, 'Did you know the rare beauty of the Virgin City, you would quickly make love to her', he envisaged what a pretty pass the virgin would be reduced to. For the rare beauty is strapped down and stirruped and day tickets are cheap, and her favours are never withheld.

The disappointment and the grumbling that accompany the annual revival or attempted revival of the Carnival have died down. Handfuls of bewildered but still eager people in masks are no longer elbowing their way through the streets looking for action. The sense of anticlimax that sits like a last veil on elaborate costumes has gone. The gaudy and the immaculate have returned their skirts and ruffs to trunks of hire shops again. The crush of costume voyeurs have gone home, together with the French and Viennese masqueraders. Yet another Carnival has 'failed'. The heart of Venice has been squeezed out of it, methodically year after year, so it would be hard for its life-blood to well up spontaneously to the beating of drums. Where once Venetians donned their masks to hide their identities as they indulged in revelry, now there is little revelry and the citizens are searching for their identity. The idea of the mask prevails. The lure of an anonymous disguise is flaunted from the stands of the hundreds of mask shops. But the masks are sold and taken home by tourists. The maidens and courtesan masks are bought all year round. Visitors who crowd into the city centre during the Carnival itself often feel that by some misfortune they have just missed the fun. They flock to the Piazza San Marco and feel the crush of expectant sightseers lit up by the flash bulbs of cameras. A handful of extroverts parade around in truly splendid costumes, followed by small groups of people decked in nylon and crêpe paper.

There is no flight of the angels, nor banquets, nor orgies. This recent revival of the ancient Carnival has not struck a chord in the hearts of the citizens, but it has touched a new button on the cash register. The whole festival has become an organized débâcle that most Venetians suffer with an ill grace. There is much more of a sense of boycott than of joining in. But then in this Western City of Gems there is little scope for spontaneity. The old order has died out together with most of its rites and customs, and the new order has claimed and cut its pound of flesh; and the flesh has been cut up and divided into miniscule portions and offered for sale at arbitrarily high prices. As always, those Venetians who cannot compete must make their way to Mestre.

Carnevale is swept away and forgotten with great alacrity. The finale of fireworks over the lagoon packs the Piazza San Marco and the Riva degli Schiavoni so tightly that the oohs and aahs of admiration for the bombardment of noise and colour is muted by the sheer crush. This last homage to the water is, perhaps, the one moment of real excitement of the whole affair. The mixture of splendid exploding rain and the crowd of over a hundred thousand people crammed into a small contained space make for a communal burst of adrenalin. However, by the following morning the roadsweepers will have tackled the

Venice mirrors itself continually. It has a slow tide of vanity drifting in and out of the city with its endless illusions and reflections. Marble and iron, water and wood are the elements that make up every canal-side café. Quiet moments are stolen from the daily rush as canal water slaps the slimy sides. A semi-submerged gondola reflects the city, literally and metaphorically.

worst of the debris, leaving only hints and traces and fragments of glass to show that there was anything unusual in the Piazza.

The balletic movement of their brooms seems to herald in the spring itself. The Carnival is an ordeal that must be got through; once it is over, the serious business of uncovering windowboxes and crabwalking backwards and forwards along the narrow alley-ways can be resumed. The plastic hairnets are lifted from yellowing geraniums, and windows are thrown open. Ecstatic canaries are put out to sing in the chill air. Along the water-ways the delivery men also sing, lolling on the thin decks of their narrow vessels to catch the faint rays of sun.

Everywhere seems to be waking up to a feeling of coquetry and display far more genuine than anything paraded in the Carnival. Each year the city makes up her face like an ancient beauty aware of her fine bones but worried about her wrinkles. The spring sun silvers the waters and polishes the surface so that each building can better see its reflection. Everything conspires to allow the city to admire itself. Each palazzo becomes a courtesan at her toilet, decking its windows with striped awnings and competing plants, while scenting itself with the perfume of flowers that drifts over the high walls of its secret gardens. The pervading scent is of wisteria: a sweet heady smell that I love. The palazzos seem to flutter their windows at the passing world, letting one momentarily glimpse the alluring richness within. As I plough through the Grand Canal, backwards and forwards on the *vaporetto*, learning the intricacies of bureaucratic Venetian life, visiting the various public offices, I amuse myself by looking into other people's apartments, at the tons of suspended Murano glass and the heavily beamed ceilings. It seems that the palazzos gaze across the water at each other, critically observing their respective splendours.

Although, in theory, Venice is still wedded to the sea, she is widowed of her power there and sits like a wealthy dowager fingering her caskets of jewels as she makes herself up the better to display the legacies of her late lord. In the peeling and stained stucco of façades I see the remains of once sumptuous gowns, trailing their wet hems over slipper-like steps that rise and fall under tides to the suck and slap of canal water on their green-slimed marble. In spring the hidden gardens begin to reveal themselves. The dark dreadlocked stems of wisteria blossom with cascades of delicate mauve, covering the dank winter smells, while the scentless virginia creeper reddens and unfurls, converting hairnets into wigs. This creeper has hung over the convent wall and its carved gateway, making a backdrop like an empty fishing net thrown over the side of the boat. Just one day of sunshine changes our view, loading it with a catch of greenery. The old painted lady warms her joints in the sun, daubing the scents of hyacinths, a rouge of tulips and cyclamen and a bright yellow eyeliner of daffodils in window boxes. A crude mixture of colours is splodged onto a master palette.

My neighbours complain of the attempts to give their city what they call 'this undignified face-lift'. The spotlights and the highlights offend them. The squared and neatened window frames on front after front, the bright new colours used to repaint the façades, the trimmed-back plants – all disturb their natural rambling recognition of the place. Yet such cosmetics seem unable to hide the underlying beauty of the buildings. Sometimes, when I venture to say as much while leaning on the counter of my favourite bar in an alley-way that ebbs away from Santa Maria Formosa, I am told, 'Yes, of course, but all this is turning our city into a supermarket. How can you be in love with a supermarket? All so clean, so exact, so finished. Where is the heart?'

There are those who ignore this inner emptiness and those who deplore it. Meanwhile, with relentless enthusiasm the tourists come to marvel at the inside of the oyster shell.

The sing-song dialect rises and falls round the endless acoustic dips. It is an urgent chattering with dozens of voices overlapping, gossiping and competing. Venetians flutter about like finches in a gilded cage. It is a busy city, a place of perpetual motion. From my many visits here I came to think how lovely it would be to spend all my time in a languorous lazy way. I imagined strolling to the Piazza San Marco and drifting in gondolas down still and silent water-ways. I imagined being able to see all the churches and all the public buildings in my own time. I thought that one of the differences between a tourist and a resident

Thrice a year the wisteria offers its harvest. The walls and railings of Venice are like the vineyards of elsewhere, though their heady scent and beauty are unharvested and undrunk.

22

The rich brocades are all shaken out of their mothballs at carnival. Only a few are owned, though; most are hired. Venetian masks and costumes today are worn less to hide behind and more to display. Right: Byron could have looked down from his window of the Palazzo Moceniego and seen a gondola glide by, bearing a figure with a costume and tricorne as traditional as this.

24

The drummer boys beat out their carnival tunes, but the tunes are unfamiliar to Venetian ears - as unfamiliar sometimes as the instruments to the players. Right: Artifice envelops innocence, turning simplicity into composition. Despite a thousand theories about the impossibility of snow settling over the salty underground lagoon, St Mark's can be whitewashed during the carnival.

would be that only the tourist had to rush around and be exhausted. But the real difference is merely that Venetians have more stamina. After the first few months of aching calves and arches, I too began to weave my intricate cat's cradle. I still have not perfected the art of jogging in stilettos that seems to be the birthright of every Venetian woman (nor do I aspire to such heights), but I voluntarily cross the city many times a day, sharing in the native impatience at the funereal pace set by foreign pedestrians.

The dashing about is atmospheric. One is introduced to it by being forced to obtain reams of seemingly useless documents from offices that are far apart and that all close at one o'clock, not to reopen in the afternoon. So day after day of the first weeks and months are lost in this bureaucratic mazurka. It seems that by hurrying through the streets one can somehow speed up the process. The thought of having to yo-yo from San Lorenzo to Rialto for the whole of the next day acts as a continual spur. If lesson one is to hurry from place to place, lesson two is to accept the luxurious pace at which all public officials carry out their work. The span of Venice's history has found its way into their slow wrists. Even stamping a document with a rubber stamp can consume the best part of an hour. Nothing is simple or straightforward. These public offices are the great debating societies of their day. Every name, noun and pronoun requires not only a second opinion but also a discussion carried out with heated articulacy by every clerk in the room. Then, often, just at the point when the relevant document was about to be handed back, it would be taken away to some mysterious inner sanctum, there to remain until the next office on the morning chain would be sure to be closed by the time any normal courier could run there. I made my first friends at the Town Hall and the Police Headquarters.

My first forays there were between March and May, organizing the relatively simple business of buying a flat. I was steered and often towed through these early stages by the expert hand of the estate agents in whose small window in the Campo San Stefano we had first seen the property advertisement. The wisteria was in full flower, dragging its supple branches down towards the water while exuding a heavy drowsy scent that stole most of my concentration from the Signora Cera. None of the fines, penalties or sanctions that she described could detract in any way from the first thrill not only of living in Venice but of becoming a Venetian. The Signora Cera described to me, with what I now realize was encyclopaeic breadth, all the minutiae of residency in a Venetian condominion while I gazed at the Queen of the Adriatic. It was only after our furniture had sat in a warehouse at the docks for two months, stopped in its tracks for want of a number of miniature and apparently meaningless declarations (all signed and countersigned and duplicated), that I became a temporary white collar worker, amassing and circulating the family papers.

Living in Venice is like being released into an enchanted maze. Over the years I too had wandered through labyrinthine streets and sat where lovers sit on the benches along the waterfronts. In my desire to know the city better, I stayed on almost every occasion in a different hotel or *pensione*, thus pretending to be at home now on the Zattere, now at Accademia, or in this or that side street. I wove my own memories of days or weeks spent in a daze in whichever part of the city I was in. I felt very much as Dickens felt when he wrote in 1844: 'Nothing in the world that you have heard about Venice equals the magnificence and wonderful reality ... that exceeds the most extravagant dream; the wildest visions of The Arabian Nights are nothing to the Piazza San Marco, and the first impression of the inside of the chuch ... opium couldn't build such a place, and enchantment couldn't shadow it forth in vision ... I've never before visited a place that I am afraid to describe.'

As in the early days of a love affair, I only ever felt the presence and not the substance of my love; the lull of a voice whose speech is indecipherable. All but the most arbitrary detail escaped me no matter how many times I returned. I longed, when away, to get back, but my memory, so clear in every other respect, blurred on Venice. My impressions were mostly other people's; I knew how Byron and Henry James felt about it, and I knew and remembered the pick-up lines of all the voluntary guides who stalked their predatory way through the Piazza San Marco. Few men can be as knowledgeable about their city as Venetians. The simplest and most gormless-looking lad will prove to be a mine of information. The stanza of dialect describing the Piazza is well known:

> In Piazza San Marco ghe xè tre standardi,
> Ghe xè quatro cavai che par che i svola,
> Ghe xe un relogio che'l par una tore,
> Ghe xe do mori che bate le ore.
> (In Piazza San Marco there are three standards,
> There are four horses that seem to fly,
> There is a clock that looks like a tower,
> There are two Moors who toll the hour.)

Living in Venice, or staying there, passing through it as one of the many millions of transitory visitors who come and go each year, is very different from living there as a Venetian. Perhaps the most obvious point to repeat is that the melting pot was covered and boiled down a long time ago, and it is never truly possible to become a Venetian, since it is not possible to share in the past, only in the present and the future. Few other places can have a past as fine or a future as bleak or the constant reminder of them from outside sources. Yet there is a

28

*O̶ur sitting room is always cluttered with furniture and flowers. It catches the morning sunlight
and the muffled sounds of the canal. Lying en route between St Mark's and Rialto, it is often as
busy as a railway station. Right: In the Campo Santo on the Isola San Michele, rich and poor alike
share the dark shade of cypress trees and the cemetery is full of flowers, tokens and photographs.*

'magnificent and wonderful reality' – but it is not the one perceived from without.

Many Venetians spend half their time rushing about across the city, and the other half ensconced in the atmospheric apathy. This latter contains an almost invisible drifting motion which has an embalming quality, wrapping itself around them with its winding sheet of fog. The lull of a gondola cradles the nerves, rocking, rocking through gauze veil mists. This gentle pace is present and interspersed with the former frenzy. It lolls back with delivery men sunbathing in the chill April sun on the decks of their barges; it is present in the rows of old ladies who sit silently gazing at the soiled pavements under trees; it is there in the lazy leanings of gondoliers too lethargic to tout for trade on crowded bridges, just as it is there in the seemingly effortless rowing of the gondoliers at work. Apathy calls its tunes and the citizens follow its slow dances as surely as the tourists bob and tap to the violinists in the Piazza.

Between these spells of inertia there are the recurring bouts of jostling, hustling and shoving. Expeditionary forces set out, divided into groups of twos and threes to the market and the shops. The customary queues form and fill with despair at the Commune with all its clerks who have an essence of apathy injected into their elbows. The modern republic of Italy has decreed that all its citizens must obey the arbitrary string-pulling of the master-puppeteer. A simple task like sending one's child to school is made into an obstacle race, the rules of which would have amused the creator of Alice and the White Queen. I have lived in many different districts of Italy, but never one with a cobweb as resilient and smothering as that of Venice. If, in sickness and in health, for better and for worse, for richer and for poorer, one survives the course, then a certain amount of fellow feeling endows one with an honorary citizenship.

The trailing wisteria, the budding jasmine and honeysuckle all belied any knowledge more secret than their scent to come; yet the quiver of their stamens in the inland sea breeze must sense and see the duality of every head that dawdles or hurries by and every bark from the *vaporetti* to the gliding gondolas. The few children eligible to practise the art of the gondolier start their apprenticeship early, learning to wield the long oar as soon as they have the strength to up and run from their 'slumberous cradle'. They start learning on the lagoon, where they may capsize away from the droves of prying tourists. From the lagoon they graduate to the *rii*, and from there to the lesser canals until they qualify for the Canalazzo. As teenagers, they will play football in the narrow streets one minute and switch to their father's or uncle's gondola the next with amphibian ease. The pride and the despair, the sense of power and the prostitution sit in layers.

A layer of sadness seems to be spread on the fine white rolls that are packed into the packet of every small child's satchel for the mid-morning break. The

*V*enetian walls are often like a collage of text book illustrations of architecture. Here, by the Accademia, a wisteria vine has escaped its prison bars to whisper secrets to passers by. Visitors may worship the streets of Venice, but the locals treat them as extra hallways of the houses, sweeping and washing them by rota, brushing and hosing the debris into the murky green canals.

children learn young and fast to channel their natural exuberance. My small son lowers his voice when he talks of the Lido: that hallowed place, that open space that smudges into the sea. Hours spent on the lagoon and *vaporetto* rides to the islands, these are the things he dreams of, the things he asks for in times of stress. From under the white coverlet of his thin hospital bed while braving necessary but distressing treatments for a month, he barters in true Venetian style. The commerce must go on. The bargains he strikes are all waterbound. It makes me wonder if the modern Venetian is just missing the water too. Perhaps it is only an inbred nostalgia of fishermen and sailors that drags them round in concentric circles, milling like termites patching up their nest.

Life in Venice is often a mixture of a grandiose metropolitan theatre and a small provincial repertory company. The backdrop is always magnificent, the players are the competent sons of famous fathers, but the plays are mostly indifferent. Venice is a great city, and I see her, as so many others have, as the fulfilment of an aesthetic dream, and so it has been. It has been said that even at the height of her power and through all her history Venice never had a population larger than 170,000. Today it stands at a fast shrinking 80,000. The only efficient drain in the city is the exodus that sucks people away to the mainland and Mestre. The discrepancy in size between the reputation of the place and its population has grown apace with the twentieth century. Over five million tourists flock into Venice each year, besieging and outnumbering the Venetians themselves. There are still islands to which these visitors rarely venture, and pockets of the city itself to which they do not go or which they cannot find; there are silent places and churches and *campi* that, although not unknown, remain unvisited. After midnight and every early morning the city is almost deserted, but in between such times and in all the main thoroughfares the tourists march more relentlessly than any other invading army.

Intimate moments such as funerals, illness or even arguments are all part of the public domain, and the bulk of that public forms part of the occupational army coming in and out across the causeway in shifts. Trips to the hospital at the Campo San Zanipolo (Santi Giovanni e Paolo), following or trundled in the wooden wheelbarrow that serves as a stretcher in Venice, are inevitably shared by sightseers thrilled to have captured a 'real moment of Venetian life'. I remember feeling resentful of a passer-by photographing my sick child thus. But I also remember, on another occasion when my daughter collapsed at Canareggio, the sense of elation I felt as the speedboat ambulance raced through the lagoon. So much in Venice is novel, with a novelty that never fails to astound, that the delight one feels is childlike and instinctive.

My years in Venice seem to divide into seasons in a way that is more marked than elsewhere. No year or even half-year has drifted by without my being

32

continually aware of the changing time. The spring has always been an idyllic time in some respects, flavoured by flowers and gently warmed by the sun. Yet it has twice contained a period of enforced reflection in the guise of hours spent in the small cafés opposite the entrance to the hospital at San Zanipolo, waiting to visit my children while brooding over cups of hot chocolate so thick it might have been dredged up from the bottom of a canal. Thus, of the landmarks that stay most vividly in my mind, the fifteenth-century statue of Colleoni is one of the most prominent.

Bartolomeo Colleoni was a famous mercenary who left a fortune to the Republic on condition that his statue be erected outside San Marco. This was against the laws of the city, but in order to claim the inheritance the senate found a loophole and instead placed the statue in front of the Scuola di San Marco, now the hospital, at the Campo San Zanipolo. Ruskin, whose beautiful prose descriptions of Venice often swing between the gushing and the spiteful, did not believe 'that there is a more glorious work of sculpture existing in the world than the equestrian statue of Bartolomeo Colleoni'. It was designed by Verrocchio in Venice but fraught with problems. After he had just completed the horse, news reached him that the rider was to be sculpted by Donatello's scholar, Vellano of Padua; whereupon Verrocchio broke the head and legs of the horse to pieces in a fit of pique. He then returned to Florence. A decree followed, forbidding him under pain of death to set foot on Venetian territory. To which he replied that he had no intention of incurring the risk as he was aware that, if his head was cut off, the senate could neither restore nor replace it, while he could at any time replace the head of his horse with a better one.

An *amende honorabile* was made, Verrocchio's pay was doubled and he was invited back to finish his work in peace. Verrocchio died there, leaving the statue unfinished and it was Alessandro Leopardi 'del Cavallo' who completed the group. These stories and so much of the anecdote and history of Venice were reduced to gossip and served with the *tramezzini* and the hot chocolate blancmange that passes for hot chocolate. Tales of the city are bantered to and fro. They are repeated word for word week after week until at a certain point (usually years later) the points of city pride are turned and used as amused or outraged witnesses to more contemporary gossip. So, after Colleoni and Verrocchio and Leopardi come the intrigues and misdemeanours perpetrated on, around and in view of the famous statue.

Gossip is rife in Venice; it grows faster than the mats of plankton that cover the lagoon each summer. The stories multiply with the harmful profusion of mosquitoes drawn to this venerated swamp. There is little privacy and a great deal of speculation. It is a place of constant rendezvous, a gossip bazaar where art and scandal are inextricably entwined.

SUMMER
INVADED

'In the summer I lie like a lizard on a cushion of thick marsh grass and vetch listening to the pattern of waves sucking and gulping at the edge of this one flat breast of an island with its sculpted nipple of a church.'

Left: *This garden of a restaurant in Torcello, has the half-wild richness of many gardens in Venice. Their secrecy breeds abandon.*

ANT'ELENA is fraught with its lemon-scented magnolias while the old and the young sun themselves on benches. At night the mosquitos hang heavily like greying net curtains over the waterfront. Sant'Elena squats on its quiet limb; by the time the invading tourists have trudged to the public gardens they are too hot and tired to continue in any force; so Sant'Elena is saved from the invading troops. Under the peeling plane trees, hot squashed picnics are spread out on brown paper bags under a canopy of buzzing flies. Despite the enforced marches of guide-books, there is a lazy drowsy feel everywhere. The melancholy and the fog have evaporated.

Every available step and waterfront, statue and seat is draped with bare burnt flesh, and the subtleties of colour are lost in the bright stark summer light. Venice becomes a resort, a holiday port; a place of bright awnings and ice creams. The yellow and white plastic chairs of L'Avena café sprawl over the Piazza San Marco on one side, attracting what little custom cares to pay its exorbitant prices and also the morning sun, while the famous Florian's languishes in a chill shade until the late afternoon. Many of the customers of both these cafés are Venetians. Paradoxically, they are relatively peaceful places where eminent Venetians meet, like ships at sea, passing for a communal coffee or a ritual apertif.

Under the mists of melancholy, created in no small degree by outsiders, there sits a stratum of Venetian society veined by the higher echelons – the scions of the Golden Book – who live their lives with an almost complete disregard for anything that comes to disturb the stately rhythm of their city. They have not solved the tourist problem, but by moving largely by water, they practically manage to ignore it. They move no further than from one palazzo to another and across the lagoon. These are the conscientious, private custodians of their vast personal inheritances; these are the gracious hosts of visiting dignitaries. Their customs and their calendars have been preserved as though under a layer of amber, the richest and the best amber. It is not surprising that in Venice, once the greatest mercantile nation of the world, the upper class is not idle, its members continue to trade. The tiny minority of families who still live this cocooned and privileged existence may be the last generation to do so with such a degree of exclusivity. Their children are already mixing, mixing and moving away; and the summer is the greater stirrer. Like one of Venice's own cocktails it draws together diverse elements and shakes them up. Boat parties, swimming parties, picnics, dances, treks to the discotheques in Mestre and Padova are the great levellers. Napoleon boasted that he would 'be an Attila to the state of Venice'. His armies conquered the city in 1797; in 1798 he ceded it to the Austrians. Long before that her real power had already gone, wasted by endless Turkish wars. Competition in trade from India and the discovery of America curtailed her commercial power and wealth, from beyond the lagoon, while gambling and general dissoluteness undermined the great Republic from within.

Despite her waning power there were spells of tremendous artistic output. The roll-call of great artists has been largely translated into food and drink, cakes and street names, but that in no way reduces the works themselves, be they Bellinis, Carpaccios or Titians. After the French army came the tourist army, but no army has been able to open up the inner sanctum of Venice. It was Nietzsche who said: 'When I search for a word to replace music, I can only think of Venice.' Although he was referring to Monteverdi and Vivaldi and the opera house, no doubt, it is ironic that it is pop music that has forced the core of Venetian society out into the open. Year by year, it is pop music that will alter the pattern of that closed world of candle-lit palaces.

There is nothing intrinsically sinister in this, nor can it be known what the effects will be, other than to provide a more united population. It is not a phenomenon unique to Venice, or indeed to Italy, but it is happening; the old barriers are being eroded as waves of blue denim lap at their foundations. I am more aware of this mixing in the summer, perhaps because that is when young Venetians go out and out in bigger groups. It is the time when they seem entirely satisfied with Venice, and when they leave the *centro storico* it is to wander no farther than the outlying islands. Jasmines, tangled honeysuckle and clusters of vivid pink rambling roses waft their heavy perfumes into blind alley-ways, and the chokingly sweet gardenias stand sentry duty outside the florists.

As a casual visitor, I thought that the summer months would be the worst time to live there, and I made plans to decamp to the countryside as so many Venetians do. Dante (who died of a fever caught during a journey to Venice) visited the Arsenale, where 16,000 men worked on a production line at what was once the world's most efficient naval base. Seeing them slaving with their boiling pitch is supposed to have inspired one of the circles of Hell in his Inferno. The Arsenale itself is now reduced to a mere museum, and the area around it has become a quiet residential area, popular with foreigners. In July and August, with a season spreading out at either end, day-trippers turn the railway station and its forecourt into an inferno, and then funnel down the underworld between the leaning walls of dank peeling stone towards Rialto and San Marco.

It must be terrible to be short in Venice, or to be a child, sometimes smothering and drowning under a sea of thighs and luggage. It must be hard to be old and unable to hurry as the crowd jostles itself down alley-ways, shoving people against the bricks and doorways and into stalls. It must be hard to be frail, vulnerable to the knocks and bumps continually sustained. In summer it often looks as if the gates of the Arsenale have opened and released 16,000 people from a shift. At first I found my nerves jangled by the sheer numbers and the claustrophobic nearness of so many people. Their excitement clashed with the natural drowsy feeling of the city squeezed by heat. I noticed that my daughter was less bothered by the crowds than I, and I asked her how she managed to survive. 'I just ignore them,' she said.

Then I asked her what her Venetian friends made of such multitudes and how they coped. She shrugged and said, 'They just ignore them too.' I can see that as a long-term solution this attitude is hopeless, but as a way to enjoying what, but for the intrusion of the eager and the inane, is a lovely dappled dawdling couple of months, it is a start. So sometimes I willed myself to be invisible, and sometimes I willed the crowd to be so on my way to the Lido and the islands. Modern Venetians are wonderful fantasists, and they are forced to fantasize from early on; living as we do in an age of television, the screen and life as it must be lived in Venice do not square.

I think I visited Murano too many times in the past when I used to visit Venice, and I have been ushered through the glass factories by too many enthusiastic guides to feel anything other than a desire to move on to somewhere else. The lure of the other islands is strong, while a certain claustrophobia seems to fuel the furnaces in the factories. The secrets of the glass-blowing that were once so jealously guarded are now pressed on all and sundry with a smothering insistence. The master craftsmen, so the pattering guides will explain, were forbidden to leave the island, and should they escape and emigrate, they were sentenced to death in their absence and assassins were despatched to track them down. The Venetian dagger was used to kill the dissident craftsmen; it was a blade made as a thin shard of glass, the handle of which, once it was sunk into a victim, would be broken off, leaving scarcely more than a scratch to show the means of death. The glass works of Bohemia and Flanders, Caithness and Piegare were all founded by the Muranese. Whenever I watch the glass-blowers making their fantastic trinkets – the long spindles of a glass peacock's tail or the sugar strand shafts of a light – I keep thinking of the razor strands of the daggers made in that island prison.

Murano has shrunk in my mind to a tunnel, the glass museum and two bars. The *vaporetto*, converted now to diesel but keeping its name, looms into view and then glides with a gracefulness belied by its size and design on to another island. Murano, Torcello and Burano are linked by the loose net of its timetables. The mooring rope is thrown and tied, its deck bar is slid open and the passengers spill out. On winter days the *vaporetti* are lonely and empty, moving around the lagoon as though looking for lost souls. In summer the ferries are full and their excitement is contagious. The grey-green waters are criss-crossed by smaller craft, rowing boats, speed boats, wherries and ferries.

The lagoon is divided into channels marked by stakes driven into the mud. These stakes (*bricole*) are not easy to navigate around, since some allow for a wide

On the island of Burano, a place of fishermen and lacemakers, the inhabitants have substituted colour for grandeur. Where central Venice has its palaces, Burano has the air of a tribal village somewhere in East Africa. Blocks of red, green blue and pink compete with each other in the glaring sunlight. Street after street of squat terraced cottages and houses display their bright faces.

berth and some are a mere shave away from the shallows and the flats that have been the protection of Venice since it was first founded (supposedly) in 421. There are thousands of *bricole*, some topped by lanterns and a few with shrines. Some of them have been eaten away by the sea and sewage, while others sit as prim and pristine as the new poles of a suburban gymkhana, stripped and tied together while the flat green sea lawn is re-mown. Gondolas with holiday-making or trainee gondoliers on them are to be seen in the most unlikely parts of the water. At the Feast of the Redentore, a bridge is thrown across the canal or the Giudecca to the church on the other side, and every Venetian who can get or be got down their narrow stairs and into a boat or raft drifts out on to the water with a picnic, wine and lanterns. The festival is so infectious that barque after barque resembles or surpasses the 'Venetian Alfresco' painted by William Logsdail. The Redentore brings out the most imaginative displays of food, lace, linen and glass. The lights and the music, the jumble of colours, wood and cloth, fans and food seem scooped from some long-since confiscated treasury from the enforcers of the old sumptuary laws.

I don't drive a car, let alone a boat, and my sense of direction is so lacking that three *bricole* might well outwit me, let alone twenty thousand. My family may sail and row and fish but I am a passenger, a happy parasite on the back of my amphibian neighbours. There is something about Venice from the late spring until the late autumn that lends even the sombre tolling bells an air of celebration. When I lived in Venezuela, one of my great delights was to lie in a huge hammock and rock in its lacy winding sheet through the midday heat. There was rarely the time or the opportunity to take a siesta there, but when I did, I perfected my rocking by tying a rope to a nearby pillar and holding the other end in my hand. The rope was by no means my own discovery, nor indeed was it one of any great importance, but it reproduced a noiseless version of the gentle lulling motion of a night train, a cradling arm, a dream rocking chair on a southern verandah.

It was Domenico Tramontin who perfected the design of the gondola at the end of the last century. Before that, many a poet and wanderer had extolled the sensuous beauty of its movement. They had the cabins to keep them dry, and we have the fractionally smoother passage, but the sense must surely be the same. If one lived in a gondola, gliding one's life through, would life revert to eating and sleeping like a new-born child? I wish I could afford to spend so much time aboard a gondola that I could find out. Alas, my experience is limited to the regular Venetian hours that we take. An hour in Venice can be anything from twenty-five to fifty minutes. It is strangely hard to argue and bargain for the correct length of time once the sensual aftermath of a ride is upon one. Blessed are the girls who marry gondoliers, for they shall inherit a great deal of money and their afternoons can forever be idled away drifting down the canals and across the lagoon. Their children can paddle and slurp at will in the marshes and the mud flats, and they themselves can have all the mystery of Eleanora Duse standing in their own funeral barque.

Meanwhile, my own small son saves up his coins, dividing the total into stacks of three hundred lira to take and treat his friends to *traghetto* rides. The gliding gondola, the wobbling *traghetti*, the *vaporetti*, the motorboats of friends, the patched and sometimes leaking rowing boats of others are all fragments of the kaleidoscope glass I love. Even waiting for the water buses, feeling the slap of water under the rotting boards of the *vaporetti* stops fills me with a sense of contentment. Whether it is the contentment of being in Venice or a natural love of the water I cannot tell, and it doesn't matter. On the Canalazzo the sun dapples and silvers the surface, flickering like a stall of fish either throwing back or swallowing up the reflections of the buildings as we pass.

The heat seeps like the sparkling Gioioso wine through my blood, the dusky pinks and reds glare in the sunlight and then, just when they seem too bright, they shift and shadow and light up again, casting more and more reflections. Half-drunken men squeeze their accordians to clusters of enraptured visitors. Cameras snap and flash, people meet and clash, thousands of flimsy gondolier hats with 'Venezia' printed on their ribbons bob up and down as though pinching people in their dream lest they should not know where they are. The oleanders cover their heads with flowers, and on the sunny ledges of dank, low-ceilinged kitchens canaries sing, and I know that I love it here with this mixture of jump-starts and lulls.

Being in Venice accentuates my feelings; its presence monopolizes my thoughts and then empties my head with a tide-like insistence. The possibilities of prolonged concentration ebb away as the endless alley-ways and the water lure me with their ancient indifference. 'Other cities have their admirers, Venice has its lovers.' I know, when I say that I love Venice, that rarely has a lover shared the object of desire with so many others; yet Venice is like the greatest of all courtesans: her attraction is only increased by her previous conquests.

Everyone complains about the number of tourists in Venice, including the tourists themselves. Henry James complained over a hundred years ago that 'The sentimental tourist's sole quarrel with Venice is that he has too many competitors there .... The Venice of today is a vast museum where the little wicket that admits you is perpetually turning and creaking, and you march through the institution with a herd of fellow-grazers.' Thus the Venice that my Venetian friends mourn from the immediate past is one that Henry James already saw as a desecration of her beauty, just as the Venice of today that I see and love is one that my friends see as vandalized and spoiled.

The Mascaron *is half bar and half bistro, with both parts tucked discreetly out of sight behind Santa Maria Formosa. A table here, in a back room, has become a part of every day.*

There is no doubt that Venice has too many admirers and, not from any moral but purely from a practical sense, something must be done to save the city from abuse. Despite the peril of the city sinking under their legion feet from their sheer weight and number, she needs her visitors. She needs their money and the Venetians need the jobs created by the tourist industry; and, probably, like any great dowager beauty, she needs admirers. At least her keepers and custodians need her to be admired. Venice admires herself continually in her reflection. The problems of Venice go back to the time it was founded. It has always been fraught with difficulties; the very idea of building a city on water is a problem in itself. She has been sinking and ailing for so long that many Venetians feel quite complacent about her most immediate dangers. When the streets are wet they ignore the water, when they are sunken under several inches of canal, they wear wellingtons or galoshes, and when the water level rises higher they pick their way across the duckboards provided for them by the Commune. These duckboards look like tables stacked and ready for some forthcoming banquet. The minute an *aqua alta* subsides, the native interest in the flood subsides with it and will be almost completely washed away by the following tide. Sandbags are sifted about with amused resignation and a great deal of shouting and ribaldry, and then life goes on.

But then it is impossible to be completely unaware of problems in the city, so the nets are cast for a scapegoat. Since the streets and canals are narrow, these nets do not have to be cast very far, and the first thing they enmesh are the

*A*nother corner of our sitting room, looking through one of the windows onto the raised convent
courtyard. At first I found it strange to live behind bars, but I soon grew used to them. This
restriction went with the apartment: all the windows overlooking the convent had to be barred,
and certain of them also had to have coloured glass.

44

Another multiple vision. This time in Dorsoduro. Some of the shops have opening times as hard to decipher as wartime codes. Right: This mosaic Madonna on Murano is one of many Venetian shrines to the Virgin. Votive candles and flowers abound in varying states of decay.

The cramped living conditions and the virtual absence of trees or gardens has bred a taste for all that is freshly grown. Salads and fruit are chosen with the same care others give to growing things. Venetian horticulture is channelled into the choosing. Left: On the clock tower of St Mark's Square, a non-committal mask-faced sun moves around a Saracen-blue sky.

48

*F*lower deliveries are so frequent that I feel quite abandoned if days go by without a florist or his boy ringing the bell. There is a strict social language of flowers here, and florists abound. Right: Despite all the centuries of being locked in by the sea, Venetians hanker for a garden. It is the height of luxury. Where there is no land, window sills or even hooks hold portable flower beds.

Drapes and flags, pillars and cloisters. This is a place of cloth and stone. It is a self-conscious city, a magnificent theatre set that sees itself as such and seeks to breed, to clone, lesser sets. Masks and make-believe, back-drops and veils, optical illusions of all sorts are the delight of the city. A smiling face suspended over a grimly silent tomb.

tourists. Thus, in the popular imagination the tourists are to blame, not for some ills, as is the case, but for everything, together with the government, which can always be counted on to be doing something wrong. Presence is guilt sometimes; when someone walks into a wall or stubs their toe it is not the fault of the kissing couple on a bench minding their own business, but as the wounded pedestrian wheels round in pain, he will see them and find them somehow to blame. So it is with the tourists in Venice (of whom I have unashamedly been one for many years).

Venetians, like all Italians, are exaggeratedly partisan about their city and their ways. In Geneva the Genevese is best, in Siena the Sienese, and in Venice it is all things Venetian. The lagoon, the sewage, the garbage and the internal squabbling are all Venetian and thus exonerated, but the visitors come from outside and must therefore be to blame. And the days must be spent in talking and complaining, which is as good a way as any of filling in the time. The fundamental problems are marked out with invisible *bricole* and avoided like the shallows of the lagoon, leaving the navigable channels that lie between them.

This is a love affair that lasts, a passion that is constantly fed and fanned. There is a popular saying about love:

> L'amore non e bello/Se non e litigarello
> (Love is no fun/without bickering)

Perhaps the quarrelling is part of this particular fault, the picking over the fabulous net, the split ends on the beautiful head of hair.

Strolling through Venice on summer nights arm in arm in the crumpled pleats of the street, with the intermittent scent of a gardenia buttonhold drifting along with me, I feel absurdly happy. Sweltering in the Fenice theatre in September when the concert season begins again and then dining late under a haze of vine leaves and mosquitos, falling asleep over a table as the meat and the world are carved up and disposed of and then waking again to the lull of conversation and the sound of lessening waves, I feel very much at home. To sit at a window and gaze out at the comings and goings of the Rio della Guerra scarcely seems like work. I like writing in Venice because, despite the constant interruptions, I like the *idea* of writing there so much that it acts as a spur.

For the first six months that I was here my time was so consumed by red tape that I didn't get a chance to sit down and open my typewriter, so it gathered dust. Now that the worst of the paperwork has been signed, registered, computerized by the state, and the photocopies - stacks of soiled voile - kept by me, my mornings are relatively free but force of habit keeps me shopping day by day. The old rivalries between the two ancient functions of Venice, the Castellani and the Nicolotti, ceased officially when the city united in the face of the Austrian occupation in 1848. Where there used to be pitched battles and fights there are now only mentions in guide-books. Stumbling back from a restaurant late one night with a couple of friends, we were all stopped by the same ghostly chill on what turned out to be the Ponte dei Pugni near the church of Santa Barnaba. But whether such things as collective shivers are gusts of cold wind from the lagoon or whether they are the sign of lost souls calling, who knows; though all of Venice would surely feel more sinister than it does, even on a grey November night, if all those victims who have been murdered there were to reach out from their watery graves.

The shopkeepers on the Nicolotti side of the Rialto assure me that the Castellani vendors are all thieves and swindlers. The small maze of Santa Croce with its silted and partially stagnant canals has mostly dispensed with masks. There are only vestigial signs of the gaudy and the tawdry in its back-streets. The doorways are mostly low and the windows are small in the damp brick façades. Shoemakers, lampmakers, copper workers, printers and carpenters have made their cave-like workshops there under dark ramshackle flats. Having withdrawn from my forays with officialdom I make my rounds of these artisans. Their visits to the bars consist of in and out, with half a pint of raw grappa or a tumbler of rough wine tipped down their throat, and then they are gone. Sometimes this alternates with a cup of scalding coffee consumed in one gulp (but coffee, they say, is bad for you if you think too much). There is no lingering over drinks here, except during ritual lingering times such as on the way home from work or on a Saturday night. My visits to them are equally hurried, in and out with only a couple of minutes to swap the state of the world or the quality of light that day. Sometimes their matchbox workshops will be closed and the 'back in ten minutes' sign hangs from their door. Itchy feet are hard to cure, the need to run around runs deep.

In the early mornings, accompanied by the water noises before the pedestrian alley traffic really begins, I sit down to write. Barring calamities, I only ever work in the mornings regardless of where I am, so the built-in speediness here is no bad thing for me. Occasionally the atmospheric nervous energy of the mornings channels away from my typewriter and into my dancing shoes and I hang my own 'back in ten minutes' sign on my door as a licence to be gone for hours, darting in and out of the morning market stalls or gulping down cups of scalding hot coffee.

Sometimes I sit in my small blue study like a foreign fish in a glass bowl swamped with food, and the fishbowl turns muddy with the richness of this new diet, the water silts. Sometimes I front-crawl my way into the huge open-air theatre of San Marco to stare and linger over a drink and recover from the cultural bloat that too much contemplation of the city can provoke. 'Thinking,'

I was told, as a young girl, 'is bad for the brain.' Venice has a strange stimulus that seems to pass directly into emotion, bypassing the usual thought processes. To wander round her, to drift or push through her is as natural and as sensuous as a caress. Her chipped and speckled mirrors seem to hold a built-in underwater reflection. Glitter and tarnish sit side by side.

On summer nights, after the bronze giants have chimed their most strenuous hour on the clock tower and Florian's has ushered its last customers into the floodlit square, I have seen the streets and sights that should have been familiar but often are not. At that hour, the tide of tourism has been sucked out, leaving beached on its worn streets only those sleepwalking visitors who voyage the city like so many Flying Dutchmen until morning comes. By lamplight the spans of all the small bridges are most faithfully repeated in the limpid water. Each puts a ring of stone on the fingers of the canals as they search and caress the city under the cover of night.

The mirroring and copying is so intrinsic that it is hard to make sense of the place. A convincing and compulsive liar will soon confuse truth and invention, and weave instead an intricate fantasy moored and tethered at all the points where disbelief might allow an audience's attention to wander. Venice rocks and distorts and fantasizes as it casts its spell, trailing on Arabian Nights in brick and precious stone. The waters reflect the buildings, and the buildings the water. It is the house of cards that took off and became a temple, sprouting like the lion of Saint Mark. Even the sacred, putrefying remains of that saint (stolen from Alexandria in 829 and smuggled out of the Muslim domains under a cargo of pork) are reflected in the decaying debris of the markets and the summer dumps of maggoty mortadella sandwiches that elude the diligent *spazzini*. Mosquitoes cluster on windows and walls in patterns as delicate as the Burano lacework. The veins and capillaries that burst and spread in a network of enquiring blues and browns and purples are miniature reflections of the network of canals and *rii* lit by all the coloured lights of Venice. The rings are the rings of dead Doges wedding the sea, and the rings of ships and boats moored to the quays and the watergates of palaces, and they are the rings that were singed through bulls' noses as they ran through the alleys at Carnival. There are rings in the ironwork of bridges and on balustrades. There are discs of watery-veined marble inset into façades. Every angle is reflected and every other doorway is hung with mirrors: scooped and framed handfuls of water.

Torcello (given by divine intervention through the wisdom of Saint Peter to Paulus, Bishop of Altinum and his flock) with its marshes and its stone-shuttered cathedral is the Venetian seat of desolation. I discovered the island of Torcello myself in 1963 when I was living in a sanatorium for children on the outskirts of London – a place that felt as desolate as Torcello while being entirely

53

unpicturesque. All the years of travelling and escapism that have followed that time stem from my desire to flee from the muffled sobbing of small children trapped like battered moths by waist-high plaster and pinned to their high iron beds. Aged ten, I was the eldest child there; and while they were mostly being treated for hip problems, I was recovering from glandular TB and was thus mobile and able to meander through the dead end channels that surrounded each of their beds in the long ward where they lay pining. I shared another ward with three seven-year-olds only, and I had a locker full of books that was replenished every Sunday when my mother came to visit me there.

I was in many ways an obnoxious and precocious child; I had spent many months in bed dividing my time between listening to the BBC Third Programme on the wireless, reading my mother's well-stocked library, and consuming comics that my elder sisters smuggled into my sick room. I read Hemingway's *Across the River and into the Trees* then, and I fell in love with the idea of Venice, and Torcello in particular. Since then, every time I have been to Venice I have made a pilgrimage to that fenland island. For most of the year Torcello does look like the 'waste of wild sea-moor, of a lurid ashen grey' that Ruskin called it, and its flat abandoned landscape is indeed 'lifeless, the colour of sackcloth, with the corrupted seawater soaking through the roots of its acrid weeds'.

On the rare occasions when I crave solitude I go to Torcello and either huddle or bask depending on the weather. In summer I lie like a lizard on a cushion of thick marsh grass and vetch listening to the pattern of waves sucking and gulping at the edge of this one flat breast of an island with its sculpted nipple of a church. It is a monastic mother cloaked in grey faded widows' weeds. It seems to be fondly spoken of but rarely visited. It is outside the mainstream of commerce, there is nothing to buy and nothing to sell. Its colourful neighbour, Burano, has its lace and its airs and graces, but Torcello has only its grim isolation, its squat octagonal church and its history. There are now both bars and restaurants, but so few that I either ignore them and imagine myself cast away and quite alone, or I find myself sitting inside one of them, thankful for their wine and water, and thankful too that they are not surrounded by stalls and booths of glittering mirrors, straw hats and masks. On hot days, by the *vaporetto* stop, an enterprising vendor sells Dutch beer and ice lollies to the incoming pilgrims, many of whom berate him for his pains. Torcello has become less of a shrine to the birthplace of Venice and more of a shrine to the American novel.

There was a time, long ago in Venetian history, when its famous textiles were sprinkled with a substance called 'essence of plague' and then exported eastwards to her enemies. I sometimes think that a similar substance has been concocted and sprayed over the luscious pot plants sold here. Given the tiny and

The door to the heart. Graffiti is comparatively rare in Venice. The same hand that stayed the powers of Europe from bombing it during the last war seems to hover still. The would-be wits are more philosophical in the city. It would be pointless to scrawl so and so was here in a place where virtually everyone has been at some time.

diminishing population of the city and the mass penchant for flowers, if all the plants that were sold survived, scarcely any more would be bought. Most Venetians are so cramped for space that there is no room for indoor plants to flourish and spread. The trees that grow inside some of the palaces are an exception. Every one of the dozens of florists sell gorgeous-looking palms, mimosas, cyclamen, ferns and tradescantias, many of which have the lifespan of a butterfly.

My pot plants move like a beaten army in retreat from the canal side of the apartment to the convent side. One by one, after making a brave stand, the oleanders and the geraniums crackle up and die regardless of the moisture of their roots or the quality of their soil. Even common ivy, which is considered a weed elsewhere, grows temperamentally through my ironwork and refuses to flourish. Only the plants I buy elsewhere, and laboriously import, survive. Hope triumphs over experience as I buy in the urbane and the exotic. I miss having a garden, it is one of the few things I miss, living here. The convent garden is largely paved, and the oleanders are tended by nuns and not by me. I fantasize about buying a garden here one day and nurturing and nursing ornamental shrubs and creepers. Cut flowers, which have always been important to me, become more so. For as long as the short season lasts I fill the flat with mimosa. It is giftwrapped and delivered from Rialto.

I don't know why I give myself so many presents of flowers here; I could just buy the bunches and carry them home; or maybe still have them delivered but not wrapped. I find it strange when the doorbell rings and I open the door and see a *fachino* with a beribboned bouquet that I feel such a pleasant surprise, even though I have chosen and bought the flowers less than a few hours previously. It seems a bit like writing letters to oneself, posting them and then opening them and imagining that their contents are new. I suppose it is all part of Venice and its layering of pretence, its wearing of masks that have grown into the skin.

There is a different rhythm to life here; it is imposed from the outside, it is both atmospheric and built into the core of things. No other city functions quite like this. Leningrad, the first foreign city I grew to know, is also built upon over a hundred islands and linked by bridges and water-ways, but it has entirely a different feel and pace. Amsterdam, which is often said to be so similar, could scarcely be more unlike Venice, given the former's geometrical design and the Nordic precision of its grid. Part of Venice's charm is its very disorder; there is a splendour in the Oriental disarray. I find the alternating rhythms as contagious as those of a video game. I find myself thinking differently; taking long slow pulls and drifting. This alternates with linked fragments. My brain races and sleeps by turns. The church bells toll and fragment the days, and more and more I divide my own time to follow theirs.

56

Rivers of wine and grappa flow daily down the local throats. I once spent almost an entire summer on the Riviera in a place called the Caffè Roma and then worked out that we, as a family, could have bought a small house for the price of our bar bill. Now I find myself spending more time than ever in cafés, watching the world through glass. As a form of live television it is not particularly exciting, but as a way of observing human nature it is wonderful. Different bars in different sites serve as alternative channels. I think if I sat in Florian's café for long enough, day in and day out, I would eventually see the entire mobile population of the city, plus millions of visitors parading by. During the carnival weeks Florian's fills with players in fantastic costumes (worn mostly, I am bound to say, by visiting French and Austrian aficionados), while the red and white marble slabs outside it fill with foreign and native sightseers who have gone expressly to look at them. So there are those inside the screen looking out and those outside looking in, repeating the pattern of double specimens, double vision, grappa eyes caught in the giant fishnet of the lagoon.

The footworn stones of the vast arcades of San Marco were designed to mark the hundreds of stalls that once stood there; now they seem more like a coloured memory; red for the merchants who grew rich, and white for all the customers they bled. Nothing much has changed, at heart, although the stalls have disappeared, Venetian prices are spiralling to the sky, they too have grown wings. The price of all things here is an exaggeration. If I sat in Florian's for long enough, I could go bankrupt. It is mildly comforting to know that financial ruin is a very traditional Venetian custom. The high prices are aimed at gullible foreigners but they cripple and maim the Venetians themselves, driving them across the lagoon. There is no tourist subsidy for the workers here.

Down quiet alley-ways, at the back doors of numerous exhausted restaurants, white-jacketed and black-tied waiters rest their tired heads in pillows of cigarette smoke. They stare vacantly into the night with their eyes glazed after another night of servicing the city that is swallowing them up. Bouquets of street lamps cast their shadows over the waiters' proud dreamy profiles. There is a sadness in the air even on summer nights; it gets caught in pockets of smoke that copy the wintry mists. Through the fatigue I think I see an inbred nostalgia in those Venetian eyes.

There are two distinct types here and two kinds of eyes. There are the dark lustreless small eyes that sit sharply in pale pinched faces. These are the eastern eyes; they have no slant, but they summon up images of Levantine currants. Behind their matt and unusually dark brown they seem to be absorbing not only the light but the cost and value of all they see. These are the eyes of the morning that dart and hustle; during the slowed afternoons they seem merely to be doing the accounts for the following day. The other type is unusually pale and limpid, ranging from light green to pastel blue and a faded grey. These are the colours of the lagoon and the eyes are much larger than their raisin cousins, less nervous; the pale clear eyes look dazed and partly stunned, as though continually amazed and bewildered while grasping an undertow of something sad. Both types abound in unusually handsome examples, particularly in summer when the dark-eyed ones are bronzed, giving more of an air of quick-wittedness than mere calculation.

Both these types abound among the lounging waters. When the streets are semi-deserted and the only sounds are one's own footsteps and chimes underscored by the lapping of water, I look into those dreamy eyes set like jet, chrysoberyls and opals, turquoise and other semi-precious stones in proud and temporarily petrified heads and I wonder what they are thinking. I fantasize that they are all thinking of the old proverb, 'Better one day as a lion, than a hundred as a lamb'.

There are lions everywhere in Venice, big ones, small ones, mutated ones, chipped and broken ones. The Venetians are proud and naturally predatory, they have no defence system. Eyes all over the city seem to yearn for the old freedom of the chase. The great claws of the Arsenale have been drawn long since, but not in the minds of the men who grew up in the reflected glory of their myth.

59

Anywhere as ornate and as finely crafted as Venice needs craftsmen to maintain and restore its treasures. Past centuries of influx of wealth gave rise to guilds of skilled artisans. The wealth has ebbed away leaving only the decay, but the artisans have remained. Woodcarvers, stone masons, engravers, printers and master carpenters can be found in their often tiny workshops.

THE AUTUMN
MISTS

'Autumn in Venice is one of air and light. Filigree mists begin to finger their way through every available space. Thick blindfolds of fog tease and decoy. The pigeon-back hues of grey and mauve take over, first alighting on, and then obliterating the burgundy leaves of the virginia creepers.'

Left: *Pigeons on a parking lot. None of the gondolas has connotations of ordinary urban life; yet miscellaneous bits of plastic covering deprive them of their usual romance.*

ANOTHER morning has cheated its way back into my bedroom with its symphony of early calls. The scraping of nuns sweeping the convent yard outside my windows seems to whisper a disapproval of my drowsy lethargy. The bells of San Marco and San Lio chime out their quarters, echoing each other out of phase. I can hear the muffled engine noise of ferries and work boats chugging down the Rio della Guerra. Soon the doorbell will ring and I won't know if it is the *spazzino* on his daily rubbish round or the parcel postman. It is usually the former, a dark and pensive man in his thirties, whose zeal to welcome me to his native city with a daily greeting is foreshortening my sleep. But he was the first of the local tradesmen to thaw from his silent indifference, so I maintain our tenuous relationship, based entirely on 'buon giorno', out of a sense of gratitude. It was not a red carpet, but it was a start, and gradually the rest of the neighbourhood followed.

Long before the regular postman announces himself with anything as mundane as a ring, he graces the narrow *calle* with snippets from his favourite arias. His repertoire includes *La Traviata* and Puccini's *La Bohème*. He is a dramatic tenor with a seemingly untirable voice. During the first months he demanded several times whether I liked Puccini, and his tone was such that I would not have dared to say no.

Outside, the pounding of trolleys beginning their tortured bumping up and down the bridges has begun on the Ponte Balbi. The jostle and strain of the street boys has been set in motion as the city comes alive, layer by layer, like a puppet theatre worked by an expert puppeteer.

From somewhere inside the neighbouring convent the sound of small children singing their daily *Ave Marias* comes drifting down. My own small son will be there, wearing his starched black smock and pristine white collar. His shoes will still be immaculately clean (they have to be or he gets sent home for the morning). His English nanny struggles to keep up with the exacting standards of the convent, where dress, in true Venetian style, is of the utmost importance.

For years before moving into Venice, I had been there for stays of varying lengths, and usually came away with exotic additions to my wardrobe: veiled and feathered tricorne hats, capes and cloaks and jerkins which I love to wear. However, within the city it is impossible to wear anything remotely resembling Carnival costume out of season. Extravagant and elegant clothes are respected and practically demanded, but the Carnival is a ritual too serious to mess with.

As I leave the *palazzetto* where I live, the various bells are tolling the time. It is nine o'clock – time for my first appointment near the Rialto. In a small coffee bar off the Campo San Bartolomeo I drink coffee and exchange greetings with my daughter. We pass, like ships at sea, up to a dozen times a day, either in cafés or in the street. The itinerary of a nightlife is dictated, in part, by the closing times of the various bars and restaurants. Florian's, like a painted Cinderella, closes at midnight. We always relocate our next day's first meeting from there. It would be easier just to go to the same place every day for breakfast, but the mystery of the city seems to necessitate a rotation of venues. During the brief time it has taken us to drink our coffee and eat a couple of *tramezzini*, at least twenty people will have sidled in and out of the bar, gulped down a coffee, greeted some friends, rearranged their next rendezvous and moved on.

The approach to the Ponte di Rialto is crammed with stalls, scarves, gloves and umbrellas, which hint at the passing of summer long before the morning mists have risen from the lagoon. We are on our way to Santa Croce, on the other side of town where we have rented an extra apartment for six months to augment our space while we restore and decorate our own. I make this journey to Santa Croce several times a day, weaving my way through back-streets and squares, under arches and over bridges, finding my way with an ease that amazes me. En route, I collect 'buon giornos' like souvenirs.

At the foot of the Rialto, on the Riva del Vin side of the Grand Canal, I mentally choose the flowers I will buy on my return. Then I push my way through the noisy scrum of the fruit market. The absence of any surrounding fields or inner market gardens has bred an exoticism in the general public; the rarest fruits are available here. The Oriental bazaar of the olden days, when Turks and Moors sold everything from precious metals to spices, has stayed, culled into this street, filling it with the scent of cinnamon bark, tropical fruit and dates. Miss Thackeray saw that 'All the pictures out of all the churches are buying and selling in this busy market; Virgins go by carrying their infants; Saint Peter is bargaining his silver fish; Judas is making a low bow to a fat old monk, who holds up his brown skirts and steps with bare legs into a mysterious black gondola .... One corner of the market is given up to hobgoblin pumpkins, tomatoes are heaped in the stalls.' Little has changed since then. There is shouting and elbowing and instalments of gossip handed across with the fruit and its price.

Beyond the richly laden stalls, a tangle of stray cats sprawl in the emptied wooden trays by the metal store cages that lead through to the water. On the far side there are stalls of knick-knacks and jewellery. The level of human noise here is so loud it hums like a hornets' nest over one's head. It has been said that 'Good Venetians exchange confidences at a distance of half a mile'.

After fruit and vegetables there is the Pescheria: a huge grid-iron gazebo built on the remains of what was once the grandest palace in Venice – the Querini family's Palazzo Maggiore. This family were ruined by their part in the Tiepolo conspiracy and their seat was designated a market and fish guttery as a mark of

63

their disgrace. Here the colours of the twelve pigments of the Renaissance palette mix into every conceivable shade on the scales and gills of fish. Boxes of live crayfish twitch as I pass, and big, sluggish sea-carp gasp in their shallow bubbly slime. There are 'silver fish tied up in stars with olive-green leaves, gold fish, as in miracles . . . .' in the words of Miss Thackeray. Restaurateurs and their minions vie with housewives and maids to buy the best.

In the far corner, away from the Grand Canal, a ramshackle wooden footbridge humpbacks to the city's oldest restaurant, La Antica Trattoria Poste Vecie, where the day's catch is served filleted and garnished under a seventeenth-century beamed ceiling edged with a primitive frieze of the Seven Deadly Sins.

Rialto was the old centre of Venice; if hubbub determines the position of the heart, the Pescheria is the true centre of Rialto. Open to the wind and rain under its pillared roof, the fish market has its own ghostly keeper. Every day, an ex-fisherman lays out a sheet of polystyrene and stretches himself out on it, shrouded in a thick blanket, sleeping or feigning sleep from five till five, breathing in the fetid air. No one has ever bothered him as he lies with his face hidden in the winding sheet of a cover. He seems as proud as the old ladies who sit in straight-backed huddles over cups of porphyry chocolate and aperitifs at the back of Laverna Caffè and its genteel neighbour the Quaddri in San Marco every day between three and five in the afternoon, decked in their finery, talking in disapproving whispers and staring down their long aristocratic noses. They use chalk-white face powder on their parchment skin. On the hairline cracks where this powder has thickened there seems to be written pages of history in an almost invisible ink that only they can decipher. In a changing milieu they cling to each other with their gloved hands like elegant survivors from a shipwrecked liner.

The day rocks gently between the two sides of the Grand Canal, stepping up and down the wide marble steps of Rialto. The crowd is a continually changing mixture which is stirred in the Campo San Bartolomeo. The incoming tourists who have trekked from the station follow each other and the signs and arrows that lead them to San Marco. They are sieved away, leaving the dregs and the crystallized fruits of this rich mixture. The more adventurous visitors who follow the less tramped routes sometimes wander around, reading their anecdotal guides so closely that they are held to the ends of their noses like giant clothes pegs to stifle the rank smell of the late summer canals.

One tends to mourn so much of what has passed in Venice and one can almost feel nostalgia for the pestilential reek that she was once famous for. I remember it, or rather what must have already been a diluted version of it, from when I first visited the city twenty years ago. There are parts of the city that still stink of drains at particularly low tides or at the height of summer, but on the

Autumn colours on the Riva Ca di Dio have none of their usual warmth. There is a sense of desolation; an empty feeling so often found in out of the way patches of the city. The heart of Venice is untouched by its visitors who scramble across it like so many specks of dust driven by the wind. There is a grand heart and a broken heart. This is the peeling face of the latter.

whole it is the more pleasant scents of the city that I am aware of. The old offensive smells have gone. The drains of Florence and many other Italian cities are far more noticeable than here. San Bartolomeo is filled with the aroma of espresso coffee being made in the bars, and there is a scent of freshly baked bread, and sweet bread, cakes and leather and a dozen different wafting perfumes and aftershaves leaving a wake of differing pleasure.

The crowd swells and thins, leaving only a handful of permanent fixtures sticking to the edges of the bowl. Someone is selling lottery tickets, calling out his wares with an incredibly deep voice. Then there is an armed guard outside the bank and a small quick-eyed man outside a shop looking expectantly at the passers-by. There are the vendors of gloves and scarves filing away their earnings with an almost mechanical speed; and sometimes, when the sun is warmest, the Signora Elena moves at her snail's pace along the streets between Rialto and Accademia, absorbing the last rays of sun, following them lizard-like from wall to wall. She basks in the fading warmth to dry the innate damp from her bones. She has lost all her furs and jewels over the years, just as she has lost her family and friends. The Signora Elena is a relic from the past, at home in her birthplace with its twinned destiny. In her moth-eaten collars and precariously balanced hats she feels in her element, accosting strangers to tell them so. This is her city. She owns it. The churches and the palaces are all hers, she says. The winter is coming and arthritis is swelling her joints. She can monitor the *acque alte* through her knuckles. She's the wealthiest woman in the world, she says (slowly, because the words catch and muddle on her ancient tongue), she is the heiress to the most beautiful buildings in Europe. We make a date to meet another day, then she slopes off after a watery streak of sunlight, shuffling towards its source.

I too shuffle on, shouldering my way back to San Lio, crabwalking into doorways to let the boys pass with their trays of bread and fish balanced on their heads. They are stocking up the trattorias for lunch. My own shopping will have been delivered back to the apartment. My small doctor's bag is full of the miscellany of an early morning foray. Everywhere I walk in the city is littered with personal landmarks that shrink the distances between any two given places. I have stayed in so many hotels and *pensioni* that most of the *sestieri* look vaguely familiar, but there is nowhere more familiar than the long dark side of the convent wall with its escaping virginia creeper clinging, bright red, with its late leaves protected in that relatively windless alley.

Every day I fumble with the locks on the great outer door of our flat. There are three locks to be manipulated; two of them have to turn over and over again towards the canal. My husband and I have our names engraved on a brass plate under the bell. We were told that it was against the law not to put our name outside the house. We didn't know then that most things are against the law in

Venice. Robbie's single rose, wrapped and beribboned, will also be there, and it is time for our morning stroll and an aperitif before the bells start ringing in the convent, releasing its temporary captives through its heavy doors. Venice rushes in the mornings and relaxes in the afternoons. It takes me a little time to alter my pace. I may seem to be calm as I sip my *prosecco* and pick at my dish of olives, but my brain is racing. It races across the square with a party of what look like Swedish athletes who must make the breakneck journey from the station and back in a day, also including a gondola ride, a couple of Tintorettos, and a bellini in Harry's Bar, while simultaneously carrying twenty kilos of Murano glass. The latter must risk the continual wrestling of the crowds, some of whom have given themselves the advantage of being armed with a suitcase in each white-knuckled fist. The delicate crystal, like Venice herself, must brave this danger of perpetual jostling. These are the modern equivalents of the bulls that once ran through the streets at Carnival time, and the china shops are all around them.

The *Regata Storica*, a fleet of historic boats which process down the Canalazzo, takes place on the first Sunday in September. As with any boat race, what you see depends on where you are. The first time one of my visits coincided with this event, I became (albeit unwittingly) a part of the show. I had been staying by Lake Garda for a week with Robbie and his best friend. They both had a plane to catch from Milan on the following day, and I had to get the train back to Liguria and the children. This arrangement gave us one day in mind, and we decided to copy so many others and take a day in Venice. So, for the space of an afternoon and evening we became three more fleas on its back. Outside the station the *vaporetto* stop was heaving with waiting passengers, so we decided to take a gondola instead. The sides of the canal were lined with expectant people. I noticed an unnatural number of them loitering on the bridge. But the usual rush of first impressions of Venice blocked out any real sense of what was happening or what the vast crowd was waiting for.

The stall of swollen, glistening figs and deeply blushing nectarines was there, offering a last oasis of refreshment before one boards the nutritional desert of the Italian trains. Opposite, the still blinkered Baroque Chiesa degli Scalzi was gathering pigeon droppings behind its boarded-up scaffolding. There was, supposedly, work in progress here. Its poles and graffitied planks were as familiar a landscape on arrival as the canal itself and the unevenly strung necklace of hotels and *pensioni*, each of which gave the Piazza Manfrin the rather squalid, ever domestic quality of a backyard filled with half-forgotten relics of one's own immediate past.

The gondola passed under the Ponte degli Scalzi, rowed by its silent gondolier. There are two types of gondolier who stand out by their manner. There is the garrulous, knowledgeable guide who can (and will) talk you through every gentle turn of his boat, explaining the history and purpose of every palace that he passes. Only the ducal palace was allowed to be so titled, all the other buildings in Venice were mere houses, regardless of how grand they might be. So the careful tourist speaks of houses where the Venetian refers unashamedly to almost everything that is to a church as either a palazzo or a palazzetto. The chatty gondolier will give you his own personal history of Venice, which varies on many points from that of every other Venetian. Even the history books fail to agree, merely overlapping like waves on a shore at certain key points and characters.

After my first half-dozen rides, with a gregarious oarsman acting as master of ceremonies to the architectural ball, the novelty of the register of great families, noblemen and Doges began to pall. The potted history that spread out on either side of the long green runner of the Grand Canal took on a slightly rancid taste which grew stronger as my familiarity with the litany of names increased. Flangini, Gritti, Labia, Marcello, Querini, Tron and Vendramin became floating intrusions on the lull of my own thoughts, interruptions of the reflected silence inside my head.

So I prefer the silent gondolier. One of the extra luxuries of living here is to get to know a handful of them and thus dispense with both the patter and the surly indifference. Alas, I have never made such headway as to gain the Venetian equivalent of a free lunch: the free ride.

Be that as it may, on the day in question the crowds had assembled to watch the *Regata Storica* and were waiting for the pageant of costumed oarsmen to pass by. Sometimes I like to dress eccentrically, and Robbie always indulges his painter's eye by dressing like a dandy. That Sunday was no exception; and as we glided along the Grand Canal towards the Ponte di Rialto, on waters emptied for the forthcoming event, I saw through the black veil of my silk-feathered hat that the restless spectators were waving at our solitary gondola as though it were the flagship of the event. I imagined my heroines – La Duse or La Marchesa Casati – being hailed thus, and I returned the waving and cheering with a wave of my own. That was the nearest I have ever been or ever shall be to personal fame here; a fraud in this city run through with circumstantial deceits.

In other years I have been part of the crowd, straining at the false starts and getting bored with the hours of waiting, often only to miss the water-borne procession through a moment's inattention. Shortly after the *Regatta Storica*, the school year begins and the ebbing classes muster their pupils. The nursery schoolchildren wear white and attend their schools all day, on an optional basis. The primary schoolchildren wear black or navy blue overalls, with a plain white collar for boys and anything from plain cotton to ruffs of Burano lace for the girls. These schools run during the mornings only. My son, dressed in his black

The chill and the damp of late November creep into everyone's bones. Joints swell, walls peel, plants in pots on windowsills give up the ghost and statues crack. The city rocks between care and neglect. Abandoned statues weather yet another winter to add to the hundreds gone by. Well-tended statues wear their plastic capes, transparent hoods against the annual frosts that put to port.

70

The logistics of the laundry are hard. Here on the Riva dei Sette Martiri pennants of washing drape the streets like multi-coloured bunting. Our street forbore ease for elegance and damp linen for massive laundry bills. Right: There are dozens – probably hundreds – of mask shops plying their trade throughout the year. Some are gaudy, some just tacky and some wonderful.

It was my dream to marry in Venice. I was going to step into a silver gondola wearing an antique lace veil that trailed behind me. Left: At night the urban Odyssies end in sinister alleyways, not with a stiletto, but a meal. Some of the restaurants are so hard to find it can take weeks to relocate them.

Artifice and manipulation, costume and fantastic faces are part of the heritage. Puppets and dolls pretend to be people, while the people take on the ritualized roles of puppets and dolls. Intricate, decadently-dressed mannequins are a speciality, as are the porcelain-mouthed marionettes. Brocade and braid, ribbons and pearls are shaped around the past.

grembiule smock with his white collar, runs the gauntlet every day on his minimal distance round the block to school. He has golden ringlets which the Venetians (together with many Italians) associate with the baby Jesus. Laden with his knapsack full of books, a miniature apricot juice and the piece of cake which is the statutory elevenses of every schoolchild here, he ducks and darts to avoid the reaching hands that stretch out to finger his curls, to the inevitable comparisons to *Gesù Bambino*.

For fifteen minutes before and after the convent gates open and close, the Salizada San Lio becomes a thoroughfare of children and parents greeting each other as they hurry along. The nuns are strict and will not admit any child arriving late. It is touching to see that the children refer to each other by their full names, as though there were so many of them that one might confuse which Gabriele or which Paolo they mean. Augustus Hare noted that 'Every Venetian boy is called Giovanni, as every girl is Maria – names which are supposed to protect them from the power of the witches.' There are now as many names here as anywhere else in Italy, and with the dwindling population and controlled births there are scarcely enough children to give rise to any confusion.

The schools inculcate a sense of history. The first page of every day is begun with the heading 'Venezia' and then the date, as though all the school books must one day join the city archives beside the Frari. Venice has always been a place, more than any other, obsessed by the documentation of itself. No wonder then that today it continues to amass its millions of documents, photocopies, computer print-outs and permits. Every time I get a new chequebook over the counter at my bank, I get a letter to tell me so. Every time I open the large cabinet in my study, stacks of documents greet me. This cabinet, which came to me by a series of wills and divorces, belonged to my stepfather's great aunt Connie and it seems strange enough in itself that this piece of my childhood should now stand by a Venetian canal. Given the bizarre and Kafkaesque nature of its contents, it is stranger still.

Five years ago, Robbie and I dreamed of getting married here in Venice. We had visions of a silver gondola laden with veils and flowers, with a procession of gondolas trailing behind to carry all our guests. Four years ago we began to make our arrangements and found (after many months) the paperwork so complex that we finally abandoned the idea and were married instead in Scotland. It would be hard work to sort out the documents needed for a Venetian couple to marry, let alone remarry, but it proved well nigh impossible for us; not least because it would have required the co-operation of the British Consulate, which in Italy is tantamount to a lost battle from the very start.

Autumn comes and goes in Venice without the familiar touchstones that I know from elsewhere. In the tropics, there was the dry season and the rainy season, each becoming as monotonous as the last without the transitional seasons of the equinox. I missed the English and European autumns of my childhood there, but I grew to adapt myself to the elongated cycle of the landscape around me. There is no real landscape here for the dying of the year. The artifice of this city is most apparent from September to November, when the virtual absence of trees stands out. There are no residual woods or heaths. Leaves fall behind high walls and instead of muffling one's footsteps in crushed velvet or laying a slippery, yellow-brown skin underneath them, one feels only the hollow tap of heels echoing on marble.

I find myself looking for familiar autumnal signs in the exotic world that surrounds me. Walking through November mists I expect to see November sights, and I still feel vaguely disturbed not to. It is not exactly a homesickness, since I have never really felt at home anywhere other than in Italy (and to a lesser degree in Venezuela), and Venice is the only place in Italy that I have ever made a real commitment to, instead of renting places on a short lease and then moving on. In Australia, the early settlers and convicts gave to the birds and plants that they found there the English names of English things, so that they might feel more at home in their strange new surroundings.

Autumn brings out the immigrant in me and I walk through the narrow stone streets, swept clear of so much as a stray leaf, pining for the countryside I love; searching for elusive images to pin and preserve my memories like butterflies in a case. The evergreen magnolias of Sant'Elena with their hatching cones and the Giardini Pubblici are all too man-made to dispel this particular lack. Autumn in Venice is one of air and light. Filigree mists begin to finger their way through every available space. Thick blindfolds of fog tease and decoy. The pigeon-back hues of grey and mauve take over, first alighting on, and then obliterating the burgundy leaves of the virginia creepers. The wisteria, which is so satisfying in the spring, opts out of the autumn altogether, dropping its leaves en masse at the first gust of sea breeze.

Underneath this Venetian palette I look for hints of autumn as I know it. The russet and ochre façades of palazzos have lost leaf-like crusts of plaster, while others hang precariously from the cracks which branch across the walls. The colours of ripening English orchards can be found in the orange, red and yellow pizzas gathered into a pile in the baker's window on the way to Santa Maria Formosa. In my 22 years of travelling I have only ever been aware of missing England in the autumn. When I ask myself now if I would rather be back in London or Scotland or anywhere else in Britain, I know that I would not. Yet it seems to be a necessary part of my own make-up to search for certain colours as each year draws to an end.

Every year as my birthday approaches I assess and weigh what I have done

This is a view through a doorway of our apartment. Ours was an ideal place for fugitives – every room had a second getaway. There seemed to be doors and doorways everywhere. In a relatively small space, it managed to mimic the maze-like effect of the rabbit-warren streets outside. The maze, the cat's cradle of interweaving light, and mirror reflections gave our rooms their flavour.

in the previous twelve months and inevitably find myself lacking. Being at heart an optimist, I am continually surprised by this verdict, despite my natural sporadic indolence. So every October I find myself at my most self-dissatisfied and insecure. I sort through my manuscripts, papers, letters, and cupboards, putting my house in order. I realized when I came to do this for the first time since moving to Venice that it had been a long time since I had lived anywhere long enough to do it properly. The flotsam and jetsam of family travel has come to rest.

Venezuela was named after the supposed resemblance of its floating Indian settlement on Lake Maracaibo to Venice itself. There each May heralds the stagnant beginning of the rainy season. There is an illness known as the Mayera, a wasting fever brought by that month, thus depressing the remainder of the rains with a mouldy gloom. The more I settle in Venice, the more I see that my seasonal disturbance is a mere mood and that the autumn here, for all its greyness, is streaked with unexpected flashes of euphoria that set the sky ablaze, and a cloud with its fleece on fire can run across the sky like an arsonist having set light to the city which burns red in every window. The red brickwork glows like hot ash and the canals are turned to molten larva. As the sun sets, San Marco is blotched as though a thousand red-lipped kisses have been implanted in the lacy handkerchief of its façade.

Next to the quick sinking of the sun and the spilt wine stains of dying creeper leaves, the best autumn colours here are the artificial dyes of silken Venetial brocades. These creaseless crumpled velvets have been made in Venice since the fifteenth century, and many of the designs that are screen-printed and acid-stained date back to that time. All the motifs of the city are harvested here, and the subtlety of their colours shimmers with the subdued hues of fish scales and the occasional brilliance of lost flying fish. In the Frezzeria, half buried behind windows so full of antiques and baroque curios that they conjure up images of plundered palaces, there are stacks of such brocades. Russet apples, Swiss plums, nectarines, olives, grapes and golden plums: all the colour sheens of a rambling and neglected orchard are there. Tucked away in a corner, airing like the contents of a childhood dressing-up trunk dragged out of a palatial attic, there is a rail of clothes and wraps made out of these fabrics. It is only a short rail of things, but it holds hours of pleasure. Every time that I feel unduly weighed down by cares or debts, I go there and then on to a tiny hat shop near the Campo San Bartolomeo, cross-pollinating the ideas that match every mood and season.

Like a snail's trail glistening as it catches the sun, Venice is full of trails and traces of its Renaissance opulence. This was a city once fabled for its courtesans and (if one is to accept the saying 'Your whore is for your everyman, your courtesan is for your courtier') also whores. There were thousands of them, including some whose grace, beauty and learning were legendary. It was a floating flesh bazaar; their gondolas were lit by red lights, and their fame spread across the entire Western world and through Byzantium. Marriage in Venice among the wealthy was discouraged to keep family fortunes intact. Girls were sent as nuns to convents where the rules were so lax that dozens of orphanages were founded in the city to care for all their illegitimate offspring. The men alternated between the noble nuns and the armada of harlots. Many of the noble families died out as a result of this arrangement; just as the custom of the easy women has died out (although the potential customers have increased vastly). The legacy of the courtesans seems to be a love of finery which almost amounts to a greed, and an inbred coquetry, and, maybe, the brazen stare from woman to woman which is more marked here in Venice than anywere else in Italy.

There are remarkably few 'ladies of the night' in Venice, just as there are remarkably few serious crimes. Handbag snatchers and pickpockets abound, drawn like magpies to an open jewel box, but crimes of violence are rare. Despite all its sinister connotations – its dark alley-ways, dead ends and doorways where in the past assassins may have lurked – I feel relatively safe in the streets here at night, no matter how late or how deserted and foggy the streets might be. Sometimes in the Giardini Pubblici there is a litter of used needles left by the city's drug addicts like thin silvered fish bones, but most of the litter consists of tin cans, pizza crusts and discarded copies of 'What's on in Venice'.

The chairs in the square and outside the bars and *gelaterie* are brought in and stacked into their plastic lobster-pot piles. The blinds of the arcades are bundled away for the winter. The blue and white striped awnings disappear. The pelargoniums and geraniums are smothered under polythene, and the shutters of summer palaces are closed once more. The firms of plastic surgeons reassemble and resume work on the massive face-lift; scaffolding with elegant brass joints rises up and obscures some of the oldest and best-loved façades. Only the cathedral of San Marco itself seems oblivious of any seasonal change. The Swiss chalet that sits on a platform high up on its main façade shows every sign of permanence, so much so that I sometimes doubt that any restoration is taking place at all. If smoke were to appear one day from this wooden hut perched on the precipice of the cathedral, I would merely assume that some enterprising Venetian had installed his old mother there, in the best position in Venice, and had finally got his permission through from Rome to put in the wood-burning *stufa economica* so dear to an old lady's heart.

The mirrors and the cycles shimmer yet again. The half-salty lagoon might just as well be a repository of tears. Sea winds blow across the waterfront, swallowing whispers. November comes and threatens with its *acque alte* to swallow up this ancient man-made caprice. The Venetians turn up their collars at elegant angles and hurry on, heads down against the biting winds, knowing that their city may be great in the eye of the world but it is as nothing to the eye of the Adriatic. They look up to the brown planked scabs on the front of their greatest building, then they shrug and hurry on. How many people have not complained over the last few hundred years about such goings on? Henry James complained: 'Of the necessity of the work only an expert is, I suppose, in a position to judge; but there is no doubt that, if a necessity it be, it is one that is deeply to be regretted. To no more distressing necessity have people of taste lately had to resign themselves.'

All Venetians are people of taste, one has only to look at the city they built to agree. The gaudy baubles are added to please its visitors. The Venetians themselves do not buy the millions of masks and gondoliers' hats, nor do they buy the glass knick-knacks. By the same token, all Venetians are experts, one does not even need to ask them; after a few moments of conversation they will tell you so. The *facchino* and the barman, the writer and the restaurateur are all experts, just as the surveyors, the town planners and the architects, the engineers and the hoteliers are. The fishermen and the pilots, the ferrymen and the gondoliers are all experts too, together with the shopkeepers and the teachers, the priests and the nuns, the noblemen and the librarians. In fact there are so many experts that no one can agree on how to solve the city's problems, so they all make a slight obeisance to these problems to show that they agree that they are there, and they make the statutory obeisance to the sea to acknowledge her presence and her undisputed power, and then they must dash – they have an appointment somewhere else; they will be late. So another appointment is arranged to discuss these things further, and the dance goes on.

Here sits an Emperor of the Adriatic with a gold paper garter around his neck. Every time I go to the Questura in San Lorenzo I stop to pay court to this indolent, pampered creature.

The Riva degli Schiavoni was the quay of fears, monitoring every high tide. Its waters were the first to flood and the last to subside. I used to think the pressing waves of its pavements would lead to the imminent flooding of our own canal. The fog rolled in across its space, swallowing and hiding. Robbie and I often walk here at night – the Londra Palace Hotel serves Guinness.

WINTER
HAUNTS

'No matter how early the hour or how dank the air, curls are set, nails are manicured, make-up has spread its perpetual mask and the marching feet wear perfectly polished shoes.'

Left: This image conjures up for me hours of waiting, not at the gondola station, but at the bank behind it. The steps and alleyways in the snow, the angled wind bites and draws tears while rising chill from snowy stone skewers into one's bones.

Although December, festoons of red ribbons and a dark canopy of cypress branches arcade the alleyways. Unlike the wider streets of bigger cities, where manufactured lights are diluted by sheer space, in Venice the decorations have the home-spun quality of the kind once gathered by large country families. For variety there are all the differing evergreens and their cones. Other places may flaunt their gaudy lights, but here in the capital of lights and chandeliers, adorned at any time of the year with the most outrageous kitsch, it is no wonder that the magic of the greenwood holds sway. In a landless place a vegetable can be king.

The shop fronts deck their low doorways with dismembered Christmas trees and lay out strips of red matting each morning as makeshift pavements for the window shoppers to tread along and be enticed by the wealth of merchandise beckoning from within. The street vendors who form a daily barrier of early hurdles on the way up to the Ponte di Rialto close and spread across the whole of the Campo San Bartolomeo. Gloves, scarves, ties and wooden instruments are the order of the day. Butter pats and meat mallets and roughly hewn bowls spill from their trays and barrels to the immaculately polished stiletto shoes of the buying glamour queens of domesticity.

Christmas itself does not have the Nordic connotations of other countries. The great day for adults is the New Year, while for children presents are still delivered by an extremely ugly old hag called La Befana, who brings each child a present and a small sack of sweets. La Befana and all her look-alikes parade and cackle through the night of 6 January, bringing her presents on the day of the Wise Men. So Christmas in Venice (as in much of Italy) has a veneer of sleigh bells and reindeer. Bing Crosby dreams of a white Christmas from the mini cassette player in the back of many a small shop, but the time is still mostly one for a religious celebration and a tremendous family feast. It is traditional to hang a green wreath on the front door, and sprigs of mistletoe and butcher's-broom may or may not be used. A bouquet of fresh flowers seems more important than a Christmas tree, although many of the latter are sold. The strict ritual of the tree, though, is not observed. Sometimes, threadbare pines will be put out for the *spazzino* to collect as late as March.

If the preparations for the purely commercial exchange of presents are relatively small, the preparations for the meal itself are not. Like the ripples of an incoming tide, anything connected with the table and the burden of food has perpetual momentum. The selecting and display of table-cloths and napkins becomes a major concern. The carcasses in the dozens of butcher's shops are contorted into surreal exhibitions. Calves' heads so pale they look as though they had been washed up on the shore, stare dumbly down at the carrots that are pushed through their nostrils while bay leaves sprout from their anaemic ears. At another butcher's, I saw plucked chickens dressed in waistcoats dangling from hooks. Some of the spirit of Carnival is transfused into these macabre racks with fancy dress and masks, feathered caps and posthumous acrobatics attempting to pay homage to the sacrificial victims of the feast.

Meanwhile, the usual preening of the feasters reaches a new peak. Out of the morning fogs that sit so mysteriously over the lagoon, shrouding everything in its celestial duvet, platoons of perfectly groomed Venetians elbow their way to work. No matter how early the hour or how dank the air, curls are set, nails are manicured, make-up has spread its perpetual mask and the marching feet wear perfectly polished shoes. Etiquette is all. Though the shallow canals continue to drag everyone along on their slow ebb of nostalgia, the past is relinquished at certain key tides. Come Christmas, everyone will wear something new. The Christmas presents are mostly of a very personal nature: people treat themselves, choosing and paying for what they want to wear to look their best for the public mass and the more private banquet.

Out on the islands, even the most ancient and assiduous of lace-makers will uncurl her cotton spools for an afternoon in order to purchase her regulation navy blue cardigan that all the wives of the fishermen have traditionally worn. Back in the environs of San Marco, thousands of housewives move like crayfish through the alley-ways, vying with each other to strike the best bargains at the butcher's and at the greengrocer's shops and stalls. There they constantly ignore the notice not to touch the goods, knowing that the warnings are not for them. Every mandarin, pear, artichoke and head of celery will be prodded and either caressed or rejected. Shopping is a serious business, a craft wherein the native craftiness of born survivors is given its full sail. Under the top layer of polished apples there will always be the odd bruised or over-thumbed fruit. Just as the seasonal mandarins, figs and walnuts will be peppered with inferior versions of themselves. Any local shopper must carefully pick her own fruits before she will then begin the acknowledged ritual of complaining about the price and quality to the vendor.

For months, I could gauge to what degree I was considered an outsider by the simple processes of buying bread and fruit. Upon first touching prospective vegetables, my attention would be testily drawn to the notice over them. In the absence of any written notice, a verbal one would be given. To admit defeat at this early stage would have meant not only being beaten, but further despised. I say 'further' because foreigners are automatically third-class citizens. Being nominally English, I was never to the Venetian eye as potentially sleazy as a Southern Italian or, worse, a Genovese. In the chest of life only Venetians themselves came out of the top drawer. In an intricate game of points and lessons, I gradually attained the privilege of probing my own buys. But there are rings and rings of acceptance, and the inner ring is only for the choristers in the lament. Life could be analysed at a tangible level there. The exorbitant prices of most of Venetian life seem to slip by unmolested and almost unnoticed by the locals. The uneasiness and the outrage gravitate around the cheapest commodities: the apparently unassuming crates of fruit, whose prices are compared unfavourably to the good old days when there was nothing but a bowl of soup for a family to huddle around.

Although the prices per kilo vary a lot from shop to shop and quarter to quarter, once written up they are immovable. So no amount of wheedling cheapens so much as a potato by a single lira, and yet the scenes of feigned surprise and genuine disgust are re-enacted regardless. Elderly Venetians greet each other like courting birds; their shopping rituals unfold like something between a password and a pageant. The dirge of change and inflation is to be heard all the year round, yet somehow the approaching *Capodanno* – the New Year – seems to remind those who have notched the passing of the most years of all that has been lost and gained in the last decades. The scales are dusted off and the pros and cons weighed in the balance. Their verdict is that Venetians are pining for their past. It is not necessarily the glorious past of the Serenissima or the supremacy of the seas. It may just be the remembered past of a childhood swaddled in peripheral pageantry. The waning rituals and the fading splendour of a city lapped with wealth.

I thought my acceptance was sealed the first time I was asked to agree; to accept that the Venice I had never known was better than the Venice that I did know. I realized months later that the closest I could come to being let into the tightly mended net of old ladies was to be an invisible audience to their lament. It is a city of mirrors and illusions, of reflections thrown back and swallowed by the drifting mirrors of the canals. Sometimes the enforced anonymity that this place imposes wraps one in a cloak of loneliness that can seem a heavy shroud to bear. But through such anonymity there is a freedom to observe and contemplate, like the invisible character in a fairy-tale.

In Venice, all Venetians are equal, but some are more equal than others. The inbred pleasure and pride of place are proprietorial. The great palaces, the churches and the treasures belong to the city and all its citizens. Yet names that once graced the Golden Book still grace a golden space somewhere in the public veneration. A great and ancient name is revered even though its owner may be nothing more than a baggage carrier or a waiter. There is nothing, though, that can beat a great Venetian name backed still by wealth and property. This is the city that worships gold. Paltry trickles of dollars and deutschmarks are not to be despised, but the admiration augments in direct relation to the greatness of the gush. Venetian gold is like the fountain-head, the source of the sea itself, the

Where the rest of Italy favours tinselly plastic decorations, Venice transports entire woods into her treeless domain. Long before the Christmas branches and wreaths decked the streets my son was off on a school outing to forage for pine cones, fir branches, holly and ivy. Houses that look abandoned through the year come to life with their beribboned garlands.

secret of life. So equality is a relative business, since none will ever be equal to the handful of families who line the Grand Canal.

Insalubrious slums have given way to a warren of miniature apartments, each modernized to a greater or lesser degree. Garish tiles now reflect the gleaming formica tops of many a small kitchen. After Henry James was in Venice in 1872 he wrote: 'The misery of Venice stands there for all the world to see; it is part of the spectacle. . . . The Venetian people have little to call their own – little more than the bare privilege of leading their lives in the most beautiful of towns.' He goes on to say: 'The number of persons in Venice who evidently never have enough to eat is painfully large; but it would be more painful if we did not equally perceive that the rich Venetian temperament may bloom upon a dog's allowance.'

During the twenty years that I have been visiting Venice, and certainly for the two that I have lived there, I have seen rather a surfeit of food and clothes, and many of the clothes have designer labels, and much of the food is choice and dear. The tenements are no longer riddled with swamp diseases, nor do half-starved tenants crowd into small damp rooms any more. The poverty has gone, eradicated with the malaria and the cholera of the past, but with it have gone so many of the sons and daughters of the city that the population has shrunk by over a hundred thousand people in the last sixty years, and the exodus continues. Higher standards of living have gathered the poor from the streets and scattered the children beyond the lagoon, changing the beautiful and much adorned face of this floating termites' nest.

Decadence scooped out the dwellers of the gorgeous palaces, leaving them empty to decay and crumble. Sometimes they were used as warehouses, sometimes not. Ironically, it is prosperity that has hollowed out the lesser buildings of the city. Most of the apartments are small now, and most are damp, but they have fitted kitchens, central heating, and instead of brigades of ill-clad noisy children, a solitary child will sit glued to a vivacious television screen.

These newly segregated heirs still carry in their blood that innate shrewdness that once made their city great. Venice became the crowned Queen of Policy through her consistent ability to strike bargains favourable to herself and the lagoon. When the old ladies of Venice rattle their newly gilded chains and long for old times, they do so with an eye to the forebears. Merchants who once drained the coffers of all of Christendom and ferried the spoils of Byzantium to enrich their city, might well have doubted the desirability of this twentieth-century transaction. Was it a fair trade to exchange their values for comfort? And is it comfort to be bound hand and foot by red tape? I think the meaning of the word fair is different here. For it must always have meant that the scales tipped heavily on the Doge's side. In the eighteenth century pickpockets

The world of Venice is so enclosed, so claustrophobic, that despite the canals, the rii and even the lagoon, one often forgets the presence of the sea. The sight of gulls always surprises me here. This is a paradise for pigeons – city birds, not these screeching fish-eaters. Venice grew out of the sea, the gulls come wailing reminders, churning up old fear and losses among the fading spoils.

90

*O*ne of the nicest aspects of living in Venice is going shopping for mundane things in a permanent exhibition of objets d'art. It is like living in a museum, and I never cease to marvel at it. Right: *Chugging down the grand canal on a crowded vaporetto, Christmas shoppers pass endless façades of window frames subtitled for the season with crimson-leaved poinsettias.*

In the beginning there was God; and God was probably Venetian. The Madonna and Child are worshipped all over Italy. I think in Venice they are given Residents' Certificates and kept in a musty archive. The convents, the churches and the wayside shrines are an integral part of city life. Christmas is a religious time here, and religion is owned and shared.

who handed over their loot to the city guards were given a part of it back to encourage 'an ingenious, intelligent, sagacious activity among the people'. A great deal of activity has stagnated. Too many anonymous reflections have floated away, not to the cemetery at San Michele, but to the mainland. The waters that lap around the green slime of every foundation, and that seem so silent to a foreign ear, must, at times, be filled with half-swallowed whispers like the calls of drowned fishermen dragged out to sea.

While the old find comfort in their plaintive nostalgia, younger and more voluntarily upwardly mobile Venetians have found some comfort in being the acolytes of the rules and regulations that bind their life. They can recite each clause and subclause of a law like an urban litany. Even the ancient games of escape and survival can be played with the new bureaucracy. Rules, having been learned by rote, can then be flouted. Loopholes can be found. Sabotage of the new system is essential, if only for the purposes of morale. The modern Venetian is the hostage of innumerable restrictions and innumerable tourists. There exist various degrees of resistance to these two invaders, just as there are parallel states of disbelief and indifference.

Venice may once have had the monopoly on many trades, but it does not have the monopoly either on grief or nostalgia, not yet on the old generation's difficulty in coping with or accepting change. What it does have, though, this maker of glass and bearer of endless mirrors, is a magnifying glass held to itself, intensifying both the good and the bad. So for those who remember the war and the years before it there often seems to be an echo of regret which rises to a crescendo as each year draws to an end. The Fenice theatre puts on its Christmas concerts, and the Verdi Church on the Riva degli Schiavoni presents its seasonal programme in its chill interior, and masses are sung at San Marco and all around the lesser churches while the bells ring their own choruses. The descant to these more illustrious choirs is still chanted in the sing-song dialect each year. So the loss of pride and liberty, and a tenacious pride in remembered poverty, all rolled in with the loss of empire, power, and more recently the freedom to be *capocasa* (head of the house) in their own home, are mourned by old men over seemingly endless tumblers of grappa, and more stridently by the women rummaging through the kilos of Christmas fruit.

The morning mists continue to drift and curl, wrapping buildings and people alike in their soft grey veils. One night, having jammed our heating system on to maximum, I found I could not sleep in the sub-tropical smother of my bedroom, and threw one of its windows wide. Next morning my room had filled with the foggy vapours from the canal. Not only the convent courtyard beyond and the window itself were obscured by the thick opaline mist, but even the room had disappeared as well, leaving me afloat in a cloud. This celestial illusion was soon dispelled, though, by the growling of foghorns trafficking their way down the Rio della Guerra, together with the echoing greetings of early boatmen feeling their way under invisible bridges.

It is cold in Venice in the winter, and the cold seeps into one's bones and sits around one's knees like a damp and comfortless blanket. It had always puzzled me before why there should be such a preoccupation with lingerie, under-clothes, vests and socks. I had never seen so many shops selling such things. A few months of feeling the cold forever threatening to snap the cord at the base of one's spine as one walks, a chill that travels from the feet through its own network of canals, gradually icing up every vein and artery until the damp seems to have taken hold of the roots of one's hair and made them ache, and it becomes clear that the underclothes are the latter-day amulets. Where once the well of fresh water that served the Arsenale was kept pure and safe by the sinking of two rhinoceros horns therein, the hearts of all Venetians are kept pure and free of poison from the creeping damp by the sublimation of the woollen vest. As with all things in Venice, the range is vast and sumptuous: there are plain woollen ones, and then at the other end of the scale there are the silken designer camisoles that cost the same as an alpaca overcoat elsewhere. There is something almost atmospheric that leads to extravagance here; accounting for one's expenditure becomes even more meaningless a task than in other less exorbitant places. Nothing makes sense when reduced to the common denominator of the inflationary lira. The vision of financial ruin is just an alluring reflection of the city itself.

The coming of Christmas has charged the air with excitement. The state of invisibility has temporarily lifted and, in its place, unseen labels are hung around the necks of all and sundry. We recognize each other like suddenly animated decanters in a nobleman's pantry. I have grown so used to wandering down alley-ways unnoticed that it takes me a while to get my wits back and answer to the streams of *auguri* that come to me from the most unexpected quarters. People are more expansive as they wait for their sons to return from the mainland and their capons to marinate in their kitchens.

My children, too, have assimilated their roles as surrogate Venetians. My son panics to procure moss for a communal *pesebre* (nativity model) and practises his responses to the nuns while bouncing a ball against one of the walls of the Campo Santa Maria Formosa with his friend who lives there. Meanwhile, my daughter has slipped into the true adolescent mood and abandoned ship, deserting the islands every evening to traipse around Mestre, Padova or anywhere else that has discotheques and is a long way from San Marco and the dead Doge's legacies. She is secretly sorry about this and cannot understand why a whole generation of people, privileged to live in such a beautiful place, crave the noisy inanity of the concrete jungle. Though she remonstrates, hers is one voice against a wave of discontent. Her peers claim that Venice is boring in the winter; as soon as they can they will leave for the mainland. Meanwhile, they migrate, recolonizing the city and the islands every summer and bailing out every winter. Every week she is invited to spend the winter in Thailand; a third of her friends have decamped there until April, when the tourists and the jobs return.

After the unnatural closeness of our years in Liguria and Siena, when circumstances and geographical isolation in tiny villages forced us to be together most of the time, Venice has driven a small wedge between us, imposing its solitude on our family. Perhaps it is bracing us for the time when the exodus will steal our children as it steals everyone else's.

Despite the fast approaching date, there is less sign of Carnival towards the end of the year than at any other time. Even Christmas begins to feel like a private festival invented for the express delectation of this city. Much of the day is dark, but lit by brilliant lamps and windows. The Merceria is no longer 'one of the most delicious streets in the world for the sweetnesse of it', nor is it 'tapestried with cloth of gold', but the perfumes and the apothecaries' shops, florists' and a concentrated mass of other places all laden with greenery provide a sense of magical transposition. The nightingales in their cages that John Evelyn described in 1645 as being kept to 'entertain you with their melody from shop to shop' have given way to the lesser strains of canaries and the high-pitched hum of unscheduled meetings. I cannot describe the sensation of the Merceria as being one any longer 'that shutting your eyes you would imagine yourselfe in the country, when indeed you are in the middle of the sea'. Yet no other town or city has the same feel as here. The sense of wonder that comes on first seeing her does not pall. It seems rather to ingrain.

She is masked and mysterious; when, occasionally, she drops the mask or lifts the veil, I feel favoured. On my first Christmas here, it seemed only natural to hover around the periphery of Venice's rites and secrets and to celebrate her feast days with friends and family. I am a voyeur of her beauty. The longer I stay, the more I see, but I am still a voyeur, I am just favoured with a cloak of invisibility, or rather the uniform anonymity that the long carnival cloaks provide. On my second Christmas here, it seemed just as natural that we should manage to slip into some of the most lovely palaces along the Grand Canal, eating capon and chestnut served by white-gloved liveried servants onto hand-painted Meissen plates. I had long admired the outside of Byron's exotic Venetian haunts with their legends of wolves and retinues of extravagant hangers-on. When I found myself on the inside, seeing the *trompe-l'oeil* green marble of his own room and the communicating halls and salons that spilled from it like bolts of fine silks unfurling, then that too seemed natural – for Venice. This is a place in which to indulge fantasies.

'Do you really live in Venice?' I was asked over and over again, 'here in the *centro storico*? Where have you been? How come I have never seen you?' I was an outsider, invisible. We go to the same places, frequent the same theatre and concerts. Each day some of us will have passed like untranslated cyphers in Florian's. Even during the Austrian occupation, when the city was divided by hate and the two factions segregated themselves in every way, Florian's was a no man's land, a neutral territory indispensable to both.

It is two days before Christmas, at another palace where there is a party for some two hundred guests, and my head whirls with cocktails and the surfeit of sculpted food. Each time my own party gets divided, I search to regroup, rambling through tens of communicating salons, each as richly decked as Aladdin's cave. 'Do you like Tiepolo?' I nod, my new friend nods round the double hall we are standing in, and I see what I had failed to grasp during the whole hour that had passed. The entire room is frescoed by Tiepolo. Invitations begin to roll in like a tidal wave. My hands are filled with visiting cards and telephone numbers. I study Tiepolo's monkey and his parrot, and take them to heart as I make my way through the paraphernalia of centuries that share the stairs. There are sedan chairs and private gondolas, flags and statues. It is three o'clock by the time we get home. A great Russian poet has recited Thomas Hardy in the Campo San Stefano under the stars and, now, a drunken foursome, we make our way home to the Calle San Antonio to dance. A voice in my head whispers undercurrents of aping and squawking bringing Tiepolo's frescoed animals to life and I am strangely warmed by the thought. Where *have* I been all my life? It seems as though all my moments had been wasted until now.

A Christmas tree in Venice means a piece of Dunsinane, it should occupy a more than natural space in a room. We buy ours at the flower stall at the foot of the Rialto Bridge.

This half-tester bed arrived with the rest of our furniture at Tronchetto. It was then transported down the canal by a narrow wherry. Whereas most of the furniture slotted back together easily, the bed refused to fit its ancient base. Eventually we rigged it and made it sea-worthy, fit to sail with the cabin trunk, but both land-locked in a convent.

EPILOGUE

'There is much of the sugared exotic
fruit here: the inside and outside. The
outside is there for anyone to crawl
over its sugary surface, and it quickly
grows sticky and catches the travelling
ant in its syrupy sweetness.'

*This is the view that brought me to Venice. Over the years,
I wonder how many hours or days I have stood and gaped
on the Accademia Bridge.*

To look at Venice through the seasons is merely a cosmetic observation; the powder, the paint, the rouge, the wigs and costumes are all that change in this city dominated by its architecture. Over the centuries almost nothing has been desecrated and little has been destroyed here; the inhabitants of Venice stand in awe of her. The laws and bylaws of the city now oblige them to do so, but for centuries this was not the case, yet the city has remained intact. During the years of neglect, when many of the great palaces and churches sank into disrepair, wearing more the costume of old grand dames than that of the handmaidens of the Empress of the Adriatic, she was, at least, a much loved old lady, and she still took on her lovers and still held them to her. Under the wrinkled mask, she scarcely changes.

I always think that it is a mark of the degree to which her admirers love her, that after they leave her she is claimed to have changed so much for the worse as to have lost her charm, beauty, sweetness and mystery, just as old lovers do in the eyes of their ex-partners. This is a tolerant rather than a hospitable city. There is nothing ingratiating or even friendly in the arrogant indifference of so many of the people who work in the tourist trade, or indeed who serve the general public in any capacity whatsoever. It is as though the natural splendour of the city was enough, and a pinch of courtesy would tip the scales too far in one's favour. There is much of the sugared exotic fruit here: the inside and the outside. The outside is there for anyone to crawl over its sugary surface, and it quickly grows sticky and catches the travelling ant in its syrupy sweetness. Money or influence can buy a lick at the skin of the fruit, and sometimes even a nibble or an ant-sized bite, but the fruit itself, the magnificent wonderful fruit, is still preserved on the inside and available only to the colony of insects that live within. Even then, there is the impenetrable core of the inner seed-case guarding a treasure-house of hybrid barren seeds.

If I ask myself where I am in this fruit, the answer must be that I live somewhere just below the skin, surrounded by the smell and taste and the feel of the fruit itself. Sometimes, by standing on the backs of the other inmates, I manage to see further than they do towards the inner core, but usually, by sheer inexperience, I merely fall off their backs and back into the sweet morass of the crystallized pulp.

Pietro Aretino wrote, nearly five hundred years ago: 'In my opinion, if the Earthly Paradise where Adam dwelt with Eve were like Venice, Eve would have had a hard time to tempt him out of it with any fig. For it would have been another matter to lose Venice, where there are so many lovely things, than to lose that place where there is nothing but figs, melons and grapes.' It is still hard to leave Venice and there is not much that can tempt one away. Those who do go often leave because they are pushed out rather than tempted. The concern for the exodus and the dwindling population grows apace. Like a small slipstream running against this tide, my family has expanded. This summer I have been wending my way through the packed streets carrying my own luggage in the form of a basket containing my new-born daughter. I dare not carry her directly in my arms – she would be jostled and banged out of them, so she wears wicker armour to protect her from the unwitting violence of the crowd.

I have sat with her, following the sun around the Piazza San Marco, moving from one side of Lavena to the other and then across to Florian's, wondering what she will make of Venice when she is older. I used to think, before I knew the place, that it would be the sense of wonder that separated the native sons from the visiting lovers. But I see now that the sense of wonder is universal, and my new daughter will probably feel that too. But whereas I bought my way into Venice, and scurried endlessly for my Resident's Certificate, she will always be a part of this part of Italy and her name is a mere addendum on already existing reams of documents.

This is a city that has always been tolerant of immigrants. The Jews, the Greeks, the Armenians, Moors and Turks all founded their colonies there. The first ever ghetto was founded here and, though it bore its restrictions, it was not the site of atrocities. Its three sections stand to this day and bear witness to the relative prosperity of its inmates. Persecution was reserved most often for those who failed to bear allegiance to the state. For the first two years of my living here I could not bring myself to leave; now that I feel more settled and my allegiance is secure, I come and go a great deal more, as do many of my Venetian friends. I have sunk my roots here in this hydroponic hothouse, and I feel a strange sensation every time I come and go: a need to be here, a nostalgia to return. I think of it as a Venetian dagger already in my flesh. To leave would be to break the handle; to stay is to learn to live with the discomfort of a shard of glass in one's veins.

101

102

The handle is falling off my favourite suitcase. It is my black bag of escape, gathering dust for the first time in years. Venice clings, like its own damp air, but I feel no desire to leave. Right: The ladies of Venice have ways and fashions all their own. The summer shrouds them with over-hanging foliage, but the winter lays them bare.

104

A gondola is an investment worth more than a house here: it has less danger of sinking and it brings in a fat living. Gondolas are kept with fastidious care. This is the gondola garage, the place where they are built and repaired. A boat yard overshadowed by wooden houses where all those involved in this hereditary trade will wind up sooner or later.